LUCENT LIBRARY OF
BLACK HISTORY

AFRICAN AMERICANS
IN FILM
Issues of Race in Hollywood

By Camille R. Michaels

Portions of this book originally appeared in
Blacks in Film by William W. Lace.

LUCENT
P R E S S

Published in 2018 by
Lucent Press, an Imprint of Greenhaven Publishing, LLC
353 3rd Avenue
Suite 255
New York, NY 10010

Designer: Deanna Paternostro
Editor: Siyavush Saidian

Cataloging-in-Publication Data

Names: Michaels, Camille R.
Title: African Americans in film: issues of race in Hollywood / Camille R. Michaels.
Description: New York : Lucent Press, 2018. | Series: Lucent library of black history | Includes index.
Identifiers: ISBN 9781534560819 (library bound) | ISBN 9781534560826 (ebook)
Subjects: LCSH: African Americans in motion pictures–Juvenile literature. | African Americans in the
motion picture industry–Juvenile literature. | Race in motion pictures.
Classification: LCC PN1995.9.N4 M53 2018 | DDC 791.43'652996073–dc23

Printed in the United States of America

CPSIA compliance information: Batch #BS17KL: For further information contact Greenhaven Publishing LLC, New York, New York at 1-844-317-7404.

Please visit our website, www.greenhavenpublishing.com. For a free color catalog of all our
high-quality books, call toll free 1-844-317-7404 or fax 1-844-317-7405.

CONTENTS

FOREWORD

Black men and women in the United States have become successful in every field, but they have faced incredible challenges while striving for that success. They have overcome racial barriers, violent prejudice, and hostility on every side, all while continuing to advance technology, literature, the arts, and much more.

From medicine and law to sports and literature, African Americans have come to excel in every industry. However, the story of African Americans has often been one of prejudice and persecution. More than 300 years ago, Africans were taken in chains from their home and enslaved to work for the earliest American settlers. They suffered for more than two centuries under the brutal oppression of their owners, until the outbreak of the American Civil War in 1861. After the dust settled four years later and thousands of Americans—both black and white—had died in combat, slavery in the United States had been legally abolished. By the turn of the 20th century, with the help of the 13th, 14th, and 15th Amendments to the U.S. Constitution, African American men had finally won significant battles for the basic rights of citizenship. Then, with the passage of the groundbreaking Civil Rights Act of 1964, many people of all races began to believe that America was finally ready to start moving toward a more equal future.

These triumphs of human equality were achieved with help from brave social activists such as Frederick Douglass, Martin Luther King Jr., and Maya Angelou. They all experienced racial prejudice in their lifetimes and fought by writing, speaking, and peacefully acting against it. By exposing the suffering of the black community, they brought the United States together to try and remedy centuries' worth of wrongdoing. Today, it is important to learn about the history of African Americans and their experiences in modern America in order to work toward healing the divide that still exists in the United States. This series aims to give readers a deeper appreciation for and understanding of a part of the American story that is often left untold.

Even before the legal emancipation of slaves, black culture was thriving despite many attempts to suppress it. From the 1600s to 1800s, African

Americans were developing their own cultural perspective. From music, to language, to art, slaves began cultivating an identity that was completely unique. Soon after these slaves were granted citizenship and were integrated into American society, African American culture burst into the mainstream. New generations of authors, scholars, painters, and singers were born, and they spread an appreciation for black culture across America and the entire world. Studying the contributions of these talented individuals fosters a sense of optimism. Despite the cruel treatment and racist attitudes they faced, these men and women never gave up, changing the world with their determination and unique voice. Discovering the triumphs and tragedies of the oppressed allows readers to gain a clearer picture of American history and American cultural identity.

Here to help young readers with this discovery, this series offers a glimpse into the lives and accomplishments of some of the most important and influential African Americans across historical time periods. Titles examine primary source documents and quotes from contemporary thinkers and observers to provide a full and nuanced learning experience for readers. With thoroughly researched text, unique sidebars, and a carefully selected bibliography for further research, this series is an invaluable resource for young scholars. Moreover, it does not shy away from reconciling the brutality of the past with a sense of hopefulness for the future. This series provides critical tools for understanding more about how black history is a vital part of American history.

SETTING THE SCENE:

1905
The first commercial movie theater in America opens in Pittsburgh, Pennsylvania. It is named the Nickelodeon, because films shown there cost only a nickel (5 cents) to view.

1941–1945
America enters World War II, again sparking a greater show of equality in filmmaking; the war ends with the use of atomic weapons on Japan.

1917
The United States enters World War I; American filmmaking begins to show a spirit of racial unity between blacks and whites.

| 1905 | 1915 | 1917 | 1927 | 1941–1945 |

1927
The first major "talkie," a movie with sound, is produced, titled *The Jazz Singer*; motion pictures with sound sweep the country.

1915
The Birth of a Nation is released, which is pioneering for its technical production and stereotypically racist against African Americans; Hollywood emerges as the central city for the film industry.

A TIMELINE

1964
Sidney Poitier earns the first Academy Award for Best Actor ever given to an African American.

1986
Actor, director, and producer Spike Lee bursts onto the Hollywood scene, encouraging black filmmakers across the country to follow his lead.

1964   1971   1986   2002

1971
Sweet Sweetback's Baadasssss Song is released, inspiring a wave of new films, called the blaxploitation movement; critics condemn blaxploitation films as stereotypical and degrading to African Americans.

2002
Actress Halle Berry becomes the first African American woman to win the Academy Award for Best Actress.

INTRODUCTION
PREJUDICIAL PORTRAYALS

In the 21st century, movies are a worldwide social fixture, with thousands released each year that generate billions of dollars worth of revenue. However, they were once a unique and revolutionary method of entertainment. In the early 1900s, motion pictures were starting to spread across America and some European countries, and millions of people were shocked by what they could see on a movie screen. Through movies, they could experience storytelling in a completely new way. Movies set in faraway places gave people a glimpse of what life was like across the globe—and even if that vision was stereotyped or not accurate, movies became the source of many people's beliefs.

In the United States, some films made in the early 20th century had black characters or showed black culture. Because a large majority of American citizens were white, and slavery was still in living memory, few people had ever been exposed to black culture outside of films. This was because most black people lived in the rural South in the late 1800s. At the turn of the 20th century, however, millions of black people began moving toward urban, instead of rural, city centers on the East Coast. In these cities, such as New York and Boston, black culture thrived. Despite this migration, millions of white Americans, particularly in the Midwest and the Great Plains regions, had never met a black person. As a result, this huge portion of the populace based their understanding of black culture entirely on what they saw in the movies.

Racial Stereotypes
Though the spread of culture is generally a good thing, nearly all early films were racist. They portrayed black

people and their culture as uncivilized and not equal to white culture. Most movies based their black characters on pre-Civil War ideas about the role and history of black Americans. Early filmmakers were not interested in accuracy. They wanted to depict black people in a way that most Americans were familiar with; for centuries, blacks were considered far inferior to whites. Early films reinforced racial stereotypes, and millions of people mistook them for reality.

The struggle for black actors and filmmakers has been to bring to the screen—either through mainstream Hollywood films or independent productions—black characters who are real, developed human beings, instead of stereotypes, and to present black culture as it was actually lived. This struggle has been long and difficult. Only relatively recently have honest, sensitive, and accurate interpretations of black America been widely available in films.

Criminal Representations

According to critics, including prominent national black organizations, many filmmakers have replaced old stereotypes with new stereotypes about black people. Instead of showing black characters in roles as illiterate servants, as old films did, they have commonly depicted them as violent criminals from the inner city. Modern films have held up brutality, immorality, and a disregard for the law as the norm rather than the exception in black culture. Audiences, therefore, are still given an impression of black people that is inaccurate and extreme.

Modern movies portray black people in America as criminals and hustlers who do whatever it takes for them to survive. This is problematic for two reasons. First, it has given white people another set of misconceptions and misunderstandings about black people. Second, black people themselves see these stereotyped representations, and some observers have argued that these racially prejudicial films have encouraged black youths to take on the roles they see on the screen. This reinforces inaccurate stereotypes.

The history of African Americans in film as actors and as filmmakers has seen movement from one extreme stereotype to another. The challenge for black artists has been to show their unique and strong culture in an accurate way, without stereotypes or racial discrimination. In the 21st century, more films have tried to accurately depict the African American experience. However, the long history of prejudice in filmmaking will take many more years to overcome.

CHAPTER ONE

SILENT MOVIES, LOUD IMPACT

Long before the rise of movies in the early 1900s, white people had been portraying black people as uncivilized, uneducated, and uncultured. Early in the 19th century, groups of traveling actors put on acts, called minstrel shows, where they painted their faces a dark black and played black characters as racist stereotypes. As technology moved people away from live performances and toward motion pictures, these prejudiced attitudes followed. Early films had no sound, so telling a story was difficult, and filmmakers had to cut corners. Instead of developing a black character, it was easier to depict them in a way that Americans understood. This generally meant making them illiterate servants working under a white master. These were roles that black people had been trying to break out of for years.

Moreover, few, if any, of the earliest films had prominent black characters, unless they were playing some kind of antagonist. Frequently, the role of black people was simply to play a certain stereotyped character. These ranged from overly respectful servants, at best, to bumbling, incompetent people at worst. In any event, they held only a secondary place in movies behind the white main characters.

Typecasting

Racist attitudes limited black characters to stereotypes that filled certain roles. This is called typecasting. Film historian Donald Bogle categorized some of these different stereotyped characters: The "tom" character was "submissive, stoic, generous, selfless, and oh-so-very kind;" the "coon" character was "[comic relief] and black buffoon," typically lazy and unreliable; the "mammy" character had an independent mind and was "usually big, fat, and [smart-mouthed]." Finally, the "tragic mulatto"[1] (a derogatory term for a person of mixed race) was destined to be an outcast, as multiple-race ancestry was considered to be socially unacceptable. Black characters were almost exclusively used to fill these exact positions in early movies.

The "tom" character was most famously depicted in *Uncle Tom's Cabin*. This movie, released in 1903, was the first of many films based on an antislavery novel by Harriet Beecher Stowe, also named *Uncle Tom's Cabin*. Indeed, the term, which most

The two main characters of Uncle Tom's Cabin, *Tom and Eva, are shown here in this theatrical poster.*

black people viewed as an insult, was taken from the title character. This 13-minute melodrama is full of stereotypes, including a "pickaninny" character (a racist term for a young slave child), the "mammy" figure, and the "tragic mulatto" figure. These characters were cast in a sympathetic light, but their roles were still derived from racist stereotypes.

Most other films of the time that had black characters were less serious. Black characters were frequently the source of humor or the butt of jokes. In the 1907 film *The Masher*, for example, a young white man is romantically rejected by several white women. He finally finds his advances returned by a woman who is mysteriously veiled. When he lifts the veil and finds that the woman is black, he runs away in horror while she chases him. The scene was supposed to be comical, but the film nevertheless conveyed the clear message—as did nearly all films of the era—that blacks were inferior to whites and that romantic relationships between the two races were ridiculous and frightening.

White Actors, Black Characters

Although there were black roles to be played in early silent films, there were virtually no black actors. The only

TRADITIONAL RACISM

Because of anti-African American laws in the era before the American Civil War, few black people were allowed to appear on stage to play black characters. One of America's oldest methods of portraying black people was the use of blackface. This is a kind of makeup worn by white actors that makes their skin completely black. When troupes of actors put on racist minstrel shows, they wore blackface makeup and portrayed black characters as exaggerated and prejudicial stereotypes.

The tradition was so strong that it survived past the abolition of slavery. White actors still played a majority of the black roles, but even black actors used blackface to further darken their skin color. A new form of live performances, named vaudeville, soon replaced the minstrel shows across America. In them, actors still frequently wore blackface and continued the stereotypes.

When the new art of filmmaking emerged throughout the country, the traditions of the stage transferred onto the big screen. Movie actors continued using racially-motivated stereotypes and makeup. The practice began to die out only with the rise of films with sound, when people began demanding more realistic black voices, which white actors could not easily replicate.

This photograph depicting a minstrel show shows its all-white cast wearing blackface makeup. Groups such as this would travel the country and put on racist shows.

possible exceptions were those hired as extras in a scene showing slaves at work in a field. The major black characters were played by white actors in blackface, their faces darkened with theatrical makeup, burned cork, or even shoe polish. Not until 1914, when Sam Lucas played Uncle Tom in another film adaptation of *Uncle Tom's Cabin*, did black roles begin to be filled by black actors.

The NAACP, which was created in 1909, encouraged protests, similar to this one, against racist films and filmmakers.

By then, however, the portrayal of blacks in film had undergone a significant change. Blacks were finding a voice and using it to protest second-class treatment in American society. The National Association for the Advancement of Colored People (NAACP) was founded in 1909, and the National Urban League was created not long after. Around the same time, however, the 50th anniversary of the start of the American Civil War rekindled old racial prejudices, especially in the South.

Parallel to these developments, moviemaking was becoming less an artistic experiment and more a profitable business venture. Filmmakers, such as D.W. Griffith, the Warner brothers, Samuel Goldwyn, Adolph Zukor, and Louis B. Mayer, had set up shop in Hollywood, and the industry was beginning to form around a few major studios that controlled all aspects of the final product. As profits became increasingly important, producers became more conservative and more willing to cater to the likes and dislikes of their paying customers.

More Prejudice, More Profits

The result of a focus on profitability was that black roles became even more one-dimensional, stereotypical, and racist. Even in the face of protests by the NAACP and other black activist groups, African American characters almost ceased to have any positive virtues or emotions, except in interactions as inferiors to whites. This development was evident in such films as the series featuring a "coon" character named Rastus, a lazy thief. Another series centered on a similar character, this time named Sambo. Both of these terms have become racist terms for black people because of their stereotypical behavior in those films.

Even worse, instead of merely poking fun at black people, which was prejudicial in itself, filmmakers began writing them as violent criminals. A 1907 film named *The Fights of Nations*, which was a comedy showing conflict within various ethnic groups, showed two urban black men slashing at each other with razors in a fight over a woman. In the 1920s, as the movie industry expanded, black characters became even less civilized and more actively aggressive toward white society.

One of the greatest influences on the portrayal of blacks in films was the producer-director D.W. Griffith. "More than any other director," film historian Thomas Cripps wrote, "Griffith gave future moviemakers a model, a cinematic language, and a ... tradition that would define an Afro-American stereotype."[2] Though his films did not necessarily promote a racist agenda, they reflected some of the worst racial stereotypes of the time. Much of his work drew inspiration from the Civil War era and, as such, portrayed blacks as the inferior slaves of superior white men.

A Southern Perspective

Griffith, the son of a former colonel in the Confederate army, saw the "Old South" (a term referencing southern plantations worked by slaves) as a society in which courage, honor, decency, and duty prevailed, in contrast to the poverty and social problems of the

Though D.W. Griffith's films were controversial for their subject matter, he is universally regarded as a pioneer in the technical aspects of moviemaking.

large cities in the North. Furthermore, to Griffith, the Old South was a structured society in which black people understood and accepted their roles as inferiors and were governed by kind and gentle whites. He considered it a tragedy that this ideal world had been swept away by the war.

Griffith fell in love with the theater, became an actor, and moved to New York City in 1908. There, working for the Biograph Company, he produced more than 400 short films within 5 years. In 1913, he began working with Mutual Films as a director and producer. At Mutual, his films began to explore his favorite theme: the romantic and tragic Civil War melodrama.

Griffith was not alone in this respect. The Civil War was still fresh in the minds of many Americans, and it was a pivotal event in the history of the country. Because it was a dramatic time of major change, it was a natural subject for motion pictures. Theater screens were flooded with stories of families and lovers separated by the conflict and reunited in the end. Griffith's sense of drama and advanced camera techniques, however, set him apart from other filmmakers. In 1915, he released his most ambitious and successful work and the film that, more than any other, set the tone for the portrayal of black people in film:

The Birth of a Nation.

Based on a 1905 novel by Thomas Dixon Jr., *The Clansman*, the plot revolved around two families—the northern Stonemans and the southern Camerons—before, during, and after the war. The depiction of some blacks as faithful servants, standing by their former masters after the abolition of slavery, was not unusual for the time. What was new, however, was the extent to which many free black people were shown as being no better than inhuman beasts. This was the introduction, Bogle wrote, of another racist black stereotype in films: "the brutal black buck."[3]

Violent Racism

In *The Birth of a Nation*, black people in the postwar South are elevated to positions of power by northern politicians and soldiers. They elbow whites off the sidewalk, glare inappropriately at white women, and drink liquor while working as legislators. A black man named Gus, the "buck" character, attempts to assault the youngest Cameron daughter, who commits suicide. Gus is captured and immediately lynched by the newly formed white supremacist group, the Ku Klux Klan (KKK). Today, the KKK is one of the most well-known hate groups in the world. Its members commit acts of random violence against black people and other minorities. In

The Ku Klux Klan, a white supremacist organization, was featured prominently in The Birth of a Nation. *Some critics argued that KKK membership increased after that film's release.*

the longest film yet made, with a run time of more than three hours. It was accompanied by its own soundtrack, which was performed in larger venues by a live orchestra. Word of mouth, good reviews, and a huge advertising campaign ensured full theaters at every showing. It was the first true blockbuster movie in history.

Reviewers regarded the film as a masterpiece, even though some were critical of its treatment of black people. The most disturbing consequence for black political activists was that many people accepted the portrayal as historically accurate, even though it was not. Even President Woodrow Wilson said, "my only regret is that it is all so terribly true."[4] Though the racist attitudes present throughout the movie were accurate, African Americans never behaved in the way the movie claimed they did.

The Birth of a Nation, however, they take on a heroic role. Although the KKK is a group known for its cruel criminal activities, Griffith's film portrays black people as the aggressive criminals, while the white KKK saves other white people from them.

The Birth of a Nation made a powerful impression on audiences. Not only was the story dramatic, but Griffith's cinematic techniques were also unique and impressive. In addition, it was

Protesting *The Birth of a Nation*

Many black leaders were outraged and tried to make their voices heard. Educator and activist W.E.B. DuBois, for example, spoke out against the portrayals of black people in the film. A writer for a black newspaper called the *Chicago Defender* wrote, "The film viciously plays our race up to the public as being one of rapists

A DANGEROUS FILM

D.W. Griffith's *The Birth of a Nation* was considered an epic cinematic masterpiece. Its depiction of blacks, however, was widely condemned and was the target of protests by the NAACP and other civil rights organizations.

The movie remained controversial long after its premiere in 1915. In 1929, an English critic, Oswell Blakeston, wrote, "As a [movie] Griffith's production was awe-inspiring and stupendous ... but it has done the Negro irreparable harm. And no wonder, since it was taken from a [childish] novel, *The Clansman*, a book written to arouse racial hate by appealing to the [worst] passions of the semi-literate."[1]

The late historian Lawrence Reddick, in fact, cited *The Birth of a Nation* as one reason for a dramatic increase in membership of the Ku Klux Klan in the years after its release.

1. Quoted in Peter Noble, *The Negro in Films*. New York, NY: Arno, 1970, p. 40.

and murderers. No more vicious and harmful bit of propaganda has ever been put on the screen."[5] The NAACP worked hard, but with limited success, to make city censor boards cut some of the film's many offensive segments. Even the most socially progressive politicians of the time were reluctant to support censorship, as it would be against free speech laws.

The social backlash over *The Birth of a Nation* ensured that there would be no other films matching its racist intensity or its widespread social impact. The few imitators failed miserably. Studios, distributors, and theater owners were afraid to produce or show them. Producers reverted to the old methods of showing blacks in simply comic or entertaining roles, but the social damage had been done. The idea of the black male as a violent criminal predator had been firmly planted in the consciousness of white America, and it all stemmed from one film.

A few years after the controversy surrounding *The Birth of a Nation*, the United States entered World War I, and motion pictures took on a new tone, conveying unity against a common enemy and the importance of setting aside differences. African Americans were included, as the government commissioned films that showed black people in a normal, unprejudiced light, such as *Our Colored Fighters* in 1918. One of the most sympathetic portrayals of black-white interaction was in a film titled *The Greatest Thing in Life*. One aspect of this film's plot was the wartime adventure shared by a black soldier and a white officer.

Changes in the 1920s

The spirit of unity brought out by World War I, however, evaporated with the end of the conflict. The Roaring Twenties had arrived, and audiences did not want dramatic or serious films. They wanted laughter and spectacle, and Hollywood was eager to give them what they wanted, even if it meant abandoning the social progress World War I had brought on. Movies grew longer, and theaters expanded across the country. With big investors watching closely, producers made films for the mass market to fill millions of theater seats.

Black actors were more common in the films themselves, but they were still confined to a narrow range of roles. Critic Geraldyn Dismond wrote in 1929 that "the Negro entered the movies through a back door labeled 'servants' entrance.'"[6] African Americans in mainstream movies were maids, butlers, or shoeshine boys—all roles in which they were serving the white characters. Black entertainers danced across the big screen, but almost always for the amusement of whites.

One of the few scenarios in which blacks and whites were anywhere near equal was when they were children. Black child actor Ernest "Sunshine Sammy" Morrison, for example, was such a hit playing opposite white comedian Harold Lloyd that he was one of the first children recruited by producer Hal Roach for the *Our Gang* series, which began in 1922 and showed children of all races playing and having adventures in a natural setting.

Morrison soon left that role, but other African American actors were selected to fill his place. Some film historians consider *Our Gang* a step forward for black actors in a time of widespread discrimination. Film expert Donald Bogle argued that racial tension in the film industry was beginning to disappear. Others have argued the opposite. Critic Harry Alan Potamkin criticized some of the roles for black children as "typical of the theatrical [acceptance] of the Negro as clown, clodhopper or scarecrow."[7]

This was the same treatment black

SKIN TONE TYPECASTING

One of the more subtle forms of racism in films is many white filmmakers' tendency to assign the role of villain to darker-skinned actors, while reserving the heroic and romantic parts for those with lighter skin. Women, especially, were cast according to color, and the practice began even before blacks started to appear in major roles.

In 1915's *The Birth of a Nation*, for instance, white actresses in blackface played the roles of Lydia and Mammy. Lydia was light-skinned and slim, while Mammy had dark skin and was overweight. Film historian Donald Bogle wrote,

This tradition of the ... overweight, dowdy dark black woman was continued in films throughout the 1930s and 1940s ... A dark black actress was considered for no other role but that of a mammy [character]. On the other hand, the part-black woman [with light skin] was given a chance at lead parts and was graced with a modicum of ... appeal. Every [desirable] black woman who appeared afterward in movies was to be [light-skinned] with Caucasian features. [Women of mixed race] came closest to the white ideal. Whether conscious or not, Griffith's division of the black woman into color categories survived in movies the way many [racist] values continue long after they are discredited.[1]

1. Donald Bogle, *Toms, Coons, Mulattoes, Mammies & Bucks: An Interpretive History of Blacks in American Film*. New York, NY: Continuum, 2006, p. 15.

adult actors received in most of the later silent films. D.W. Griffith did not make another film portraying African Americans as violently as he did in *The Birth of a Nation*, but he still made films such as 1922's *One Exciting Night*, in which a white actor in blackface plays Romeo Washington, a butler whose eyes bug out while in a haunted house and who,

Bogle wrote, was "a racially crude and self-demeaning character."[8]

Some Kind of Progress

Mainstream movie parts were increasingly available to black actors in the 1920s. However, apart from uncivilized savages in jungle adventure films, happy and respectful servants were the only roles for blacks at this time in Hollywood. Thoughtful and equal portrayals of black people were rare for two reasons. First, large production companies were terrified of offending their mainly white audiences. It was easy to please most white people at the time by using black stereotypes, and anything else could have hurt their profits. Second, the film industry had rules that were intended to censor inappropriate films, and depicting racial equality was a bold and controversial topic at the time.

With no new black themes to pursue, filmmakers returned to the old ones. The silent era ended with the 1927 remake of *Uncle Tom's Cabin*, and the casting of the Uncle Tom role showed both how little and how much progress had been made since 1903. Acclaimed black stage actor Charles Gilpin was signed for the part, but he was fired because his portrayal was considered too aggressive. John B. Lowe, also a black actor, took on the role, and his performance stood out enough from previous film adaptations that critic Edith Isaacs wrote that his character "seems to wear his ball and chain with a difference."[9]

Later in 1927, the first major sound film, *The Jazz Singer*, was released. This marked a significant step forward in entertainment technologies. Movies that now had sound were called "talkies," and they gave audiences a taste for realism that would spell the end of blackface and pave the way for Hollywood's first black stars. *The Jazz Singer* itself, however, featured a white actor named Al Jolson in blackface singing a song titled "Mammy." African Americans had certainly made strides from the turn of the century, but equality, whether in the film industry or in America as a whole, was still far from reality.

CHAPTER TWO
THE RISE OF AFRICAN AMERICANS IN HOLLYWOOD

For African Americans, the early years of the film industry were just as prejudicial and racist as the national mood of the early 1900s. Millions of Americans still firmly believed in the old, discriminatory practices of pre-Civil War society, and movies were made to reinforce those ideas. Though there was a brief period of racial unity during World War I, the progress of black people in the movie industry was slow and painful.

Serious movies about African Americans in the silent film era were few and far between. These films about genuine and realistic African American experiences were also underfunded. Though interactions with black people were increasingly a part of everyday life for most Americans, the entertainment industry still found it easier—and more profitable—to play into outdated and racist stereotypes. As the industry expanded, directors and producers were less willing to take risks, and they certainly did not want to lose their job for suggesting a movie with equal black and white actors. Moreover, the rare African American that was employed as a producer or director was unable to get any mainstream support for their work.

The first film created specifically to appeal to black viewers, a genre called "race movies" at the time, was named *The Railroad Porter* (or *The Pullman Porter*) and produced in 1912. Not much information survives about this film, which shows how unsuccessful its original run was. In fact, it was not until 1915's *The Birth of a Nation* that there was a significant push toward making movies for—and by—African Americans. As part of the backlash from that film's portrayal of black people, activist organizations, such as the NAACP, demanded that Hollywood produce a movie that would provide more appropriate representation.

WHAT IT WAS LIKE

Ossie Davis, a distinguished black actor who appeared in more than 40 films and directed *Cotton Comes to Harlem* in 1970, died in 2005 at the age of 87. He was old enough to remember having seen "race movies" in the 1920s and 1930s, and recalled the experience:

> *There were black people behind the scenes, telling our black story to us as we sat in black theaters. We listened blackly, and a beautiful thing happened to us as we saw ourselves up on the screen. We knew that sometimes it was awkward, that sometimes the films behaved differently than the ones we saw in the white theater. It didn't matter. It was ours, and even the mistakes were ours, and the fools were ours, and the villains were ours, and the people who won were ours, and the losers were ours. We were comforted by that knowledge as we sat in the dark, knowing that there was something about us up there on that screen, controlled by us, created by us—our own image, as we saw ourselves.*[1]

Ossie Davis was a groundbreaking African American in the motion picture industry. He was a hugely successful actor and eventually became a director.

1. Quoted in Allyson Nadia Field, *Uplift Cinema: The Emergence of African American Film and the Possibility of Black Modernity.* Durham, NC: Duke University Press, 2015.

In response to these protests, one of the largest movie studios at the time, Universal, offered to put up $60,000 toward producing such a film, titled *Lincoln's Dream*, if the NAACP could raise an additional $50,000. The activist group could not raise the funds, and Universal Studios eventually backed out of the arrangement. Racially equal movies would have to come from another source.

Activists Acting Out

Prominent African American educator Booker T. Washington and his personal secretary, Emmett J. Scott, began looking for ways to form a black-controlled film organization. One of their ideas was to bring Washington's autobiography *Up from Slavery* to the big screen. Such an undertaking, Scott wrote, would show "not only Dr. Washington's personal strivings, but also the strivings of the race climbing up from the tragic period represented by slavery in America."[10]

The project had not yet begun when Washington died, which caused many investors to lose interest. Scott, however, had once been approached about participating in the filming of *Lincoln's Dream*. He resurrected that project, signed a contract with a film company in Chicago owned by Edwin L. Barker, and set about seeking more investors.

However, the contract for *Lincoln's Dream*, which would be retitled *The Birth of a Race*, allowed Barker to sell control of the film to William Selig, a filmmaker in Los Angeles. Scott had some success raising his own money for the project, but when the film was only half finished after two years and more than $100,000, Selig backed out, and the project was taken over by yet another production manager, Daniel Frohman. Scott and his partners, who had wanted to create a film to uplift the spirit of African Americans, no longer had creative control.

The Birth of a Race was eventually completed, but it had almost no resemblance to Washington, Scott, and the NAACP's original vision. A long prologue was added, but it had no relation to film footage that had already been shot. By the end of production, much of the footage featuring black people was eliminated, and the film was turned into a World War I propaganda piece. It premiered in 1918 and was a complete disaster. *Variety* magazine called it "the most grotesque cinema [creation] in the history of the picture business."[11]

Innovative Brothers

George Perry Johnson, a postal worker in Omaha, Nebraska, had watched the failures of black filmmakers carefully. Johnson and his brother Noble, a black actor who appeared in a number of movies in the early 1900s, formed the Lincoln Motion Picture Company together in 1916. The Johnsons were convinced that a growing black urban market would support their films. George Johnson wrote that he would "picture the Negro as he is in his every day life, a human being with human [tendencies], and one of talent and intellect."[12]

He was determined that his company would avoid the mistakes of others, which he believed were caused by a dependence on white investors, studios, and distributors. He set up his own network of film professionals, making contacts with black journalists, distributors, and theater owners throughout the country.

The company's first film, released in 1916, was titled *The Realization of a Negro's Ambition*, and it had a run time of 20 minutes. It featured a black main character played by a black actor, a young man whose persistence and hard work eventually make him wealthy and enable him to marry his girlfriend. The film was a success with both critics and audiences. Though classified as a race movie, it was one of the first motion pictures in history to truly give African American characters a chance to be more than racial stereotypes. The story was dramatic instead of comical, and there was a strong plotline connecting everything together. As of 2017, however, the film has been lost.

The Realization of a Negro's Ambition made money for the Lincoln Motion Picture Company, but not enough to fully finance its next film. Between what George could raise and what Noble earned as an actor, they were able to produce a second film by 1918, this one named *The Trooper of Troop K*. Noble Johnson played the lead role as a young man who cannot keep a job and who, at the urging of his girlfriend, joins the army. There, he gets a new attitude, distinguishes himself in battle, and eventually returns home to marry his sweetheart.

Money Problems

The Trooper of Troop K was just as successful as the Johnsons' first film. It played to a long string of sold-out shows at urban black theaters in California. It also moved to other states and sold out shows to mixed-race audiences in normally whites-only theaters. The profits, however, were still short of what was needed to produce another film, and raising money proved even more difficult than before.

In this regard, the Johnsons were victims of their own prosperity. As their first two films received critical and commercial success, rival film companies started to spring up. These companies drew away some investors from the already limited pool of money available for investment in race movies. Two of the biggest companies among these investors were the white-owned Reol

AUTHOR AND FILMMAKER

Oscar Micheaux was a famous African American author and filmmaker. He first rose to prominence by writing novels, which he later adapted into a number of films through his Micheaux Film Corporation in the 1920s and 1930s. Many of his films were popular among both blacks and whites. He had a good reason to write, produce, and adapt his own novels, which he explained in 1951:

> I want to see the Negro pictured in books [and movies] just like he lives. But, if you write that way, the white book publishers won't publish your scripts, so I formed my own book publishing firm and write my own books, and Negroes like them, too, because three of them are best sellers.[1]

1. Quoted in Kansas Historical Society, "Oscar Micheaux," Kansapedia, last modified January 2016. www.kshs.org/kansapedia/oscar-micheaux/17713Oscar.

Productions Company of New York and Ebony Pictures, a company run by black filmmaker Luther J. Pollard. Pollard boasted that his films were made "without those [racist] situations which are usually attributed to the American Negro,"[13] but his comedies still included the same old stereotypes. Many of their films were unsuccessful at the box office because black people did not want to support discriminatory films, and white people did not want to support a black film company.

Whatever their faults, Reol and Ebony at least did produce motion pictures. A number of companies raised funds by promising expensive, professional productions that were never made. George Johnson studied and kept a record of these numerous scam companies. He collected copies of their slick, glossy brochures, on which he wrote "no records of any film produced."[14]

Other factors worked against the Lincoln Company when it tried to raise funds. A postwar economic recession, which hit after World War I, meant that most Americans, especially black people, had less money to spend at the theater. A nationwide influenza epidemic also reduced audiences across the country. Universal Studios, the company for which Noble Johnson did much of his acting work, told him that if he wanted to continue working for them, he could no longer make pictures for Lincoln.

Short-Lived Lincoln

Despite these significant setbacks, Lincoln would go on to produce two more films—*A Man's Duty* in 1919 and *By Right of Birth* in 1921. Though these films were generally considered to be critically successful, they failed financially. The doors to the Lincoln Motion Picture Company closed in the early 1920s. Thomas Cripps wrote that Lincoln had "provided a black [artistic] statement where otherwise there would have been a void; it ... demonstrated possibilities."[15] Though it lasted fewer than 10 years, Lincoln proved that the American dream of prosperity and upward mobility was starting to be available to black people. Moreover, through their own hard work and determination, the Johnson brothers proved that African Americans could overcome barriers, even those created by the white majority.

Of the Johnsons' many rivals, the most significant—and the one who finally took their place as the nation's leading black filmmaker—was a man named Oscar Micheaux. One of 13 children of parents who were former slaves, Micheaux was raised in Kansas. At the age of 21, he established a farm in South Dakota, an area that was overwhelmingly white. He recorded his experience in his first novel, *The Conquest*, published in 1913. He initially sold copies of it door-to-door to neighboring white farmers and in nearby towns.

In 1915, after losing his farm due to a severe drought, Micheaux moved to Sioux City, Iowa, where he established the Western Book and

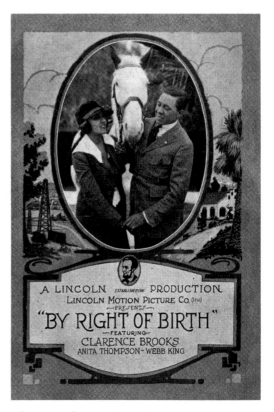

The Lincoln Motion Picture Company, founded by George and Noble Johnson, produced a number of movies that featured successful and realistic African American characters. By Right of Birth was one of their later films.

Supply Company. He rewrote his original novel, retitled it *The Homesteader*, and sold it door-to-door throughout the Midwest. In early 1918, the Johnson brothers read the book and thought it would make an ideal film for their company.

When they approached Micheaux to negotiate a contract to adapt the book into a film, however, they could not come to an agreement. Micheaux insisted on directing the film himself, and he demanded that it be created with a big budget. Because the Lincoln Motion Picture Company could not concede either of these points, they gave up trying to create the movie. Micheaux then set out to make the film on his own. He moved to Chicago, Illinois, and reorganized his company as the Micheaux Film Corporation. To raise funds, he turned to the midwestern farmers and merchants who had bought his original book. He sold them stock in his new company, and this raised enough money for his film project.

With speed and confidence that both impressed and intimidated George Johnson, who called Micheaux "a rough Negro who got his hands on some cash,"[16] Micheaux filmed *The Homesteader* and scheduled its Chicago debut for 1919. Micheaux was a relentless promoter. His prerelease advertisement in a Chicago newspaper boasted that the film was "destined to mark a new epoch [era] in the achievements of the Darker Races."[17] One of the promotional brochures he used to raise money promised that "nothing would make more people anxious to see a picture than a [poster] reading: 'SHALL RACES INTERMARRY.'"[18]

Whether it was because of the quality of the film or the extent of promotion, *The Homesteader* was a financial success. Micheaux was able to do what the Johnson brothers had not: He made enough money to fully finance his next project, a movie titled *Within Our Gates*. He based this film on the case of Leo Frank, a Jewish man lynched by a Georgia mob in 1915, and rewrote it as the story of the lynching of a black farmer who was unjustly accused of murder.

Difficulty Opening

Within Our Gates premiered in 1920 at Chicago's Vendome Theater, but not without facing its own challenges. Chicago had experienced a race riot a few months before, and many city leaders believed the film's sensitive subject matter could easily spark more violence. The Chicago Board of Movie Censors tried to block its release. City officials

A CONTROVERSIAL CAREER

Oscar Micheaux was the most successful producer of race movies in the 1920s. Micheaux was frequently criticized, however, for concentrating on middle-class black issues while ignoring the reality of millions of impoverished African Americans. Film history expert Donald Bogle evaluated Micheaux:

What remains Oscar Micheaux's greatest contribution ... is often viewed by contemporary black audiences as his severest short-coming. That his films reflected the interests and outlooks of the black bourgeoisie [middle class] will no doubt always be held against him. His films never centered on the ghetto; they [rarely] dealt with racial misery and decay. Instead they concentrated on the ... difficulties facing "professional people." But to appreciate Micheaux's films one must understand that he was moving as far as possible away from Hollywood's [stereotypical] jesters and servants. He wanted to give his audience something to further the race, not hinder it.[1]

Oscar Micheaux was one of the first great African American filmmakers. Though his work was sometimes controversial, he succeeded where many others had failed.

1. Quoted in Columbus Salley, *The Black 100: A Ranking of the Most Influential African-Americans, Past and Present.* New York, NY: Kensington, 1999, p. 296.

convinced the censors to change their decision, and it was able to premiere on schedule.

Despite the controversy, which made it into the papers, and Micheaux's steady stream of promotion, *Within Our Gates* was not as successful as his first film. The lynching theme discouraged theater owners and distributors, and the film received almost no screenings in the South, where the white majority did not want to show a movie that spoke out against racism.

Micheaux's next film was received quite well. Released in 1920, *The Brute* starred black boxer Sam Langford. He had another hit with *Body and Soul* in 1925. *Body and Soul* was particularly noteworthy for several reasons. It marked the screen debut of black acting star Paul Robeson. It is one of Micheaux's few films set in a poor, mainly-black neighborhood. It showed corruption and black people taking advantage of each other; the main character is a phony minister who steals and commits murder.

Many of Micheaux's films were not considered intellectual and original. A number of them openly copied standard white themes of the time. He even advertised his star actors as copies, calling them things such as the "black [Rudolph] Valentino," a famous white actor, or the "Negro [Jean] Harlow,"[19] a famous actress. Furthermore, many of his featured actors were light-skinned, leading some people to criticize his casting choices.

Not a Lot to Spend

As far as the technical aspect of film-making goes, Micheaux's films were relatively unsophisticated, even less so than *The Birth of a Nation*, which was nearly a decade old. Many historians argue that his work was not technically complex because he simply did not have the huge budgets that white-run Hollywood studios worked with. As a result, he needed to allocate his funds more efficiently. He could not afford to hire the best camera operators, set designers, or stage crews in the business. Instead, his films tried to draw focus through their stories and themes of racism in America.

Near the end of the 1920s, Micheaux was also facing new competition. A group named the Colored Players Film Corporation went into production in Philadelphia, Pennsylvania, and other competitors in the film industry led to an eventual decline in Micheaux's popularity across the country. He continued to make moves into the 1940s, but none of them were as successful as his first few attempts. Micheaux was the first black filmmaker to produce a feature-length movie with sound, and though it did not become a box office success, he continued his groundbreaking work until he was forced out of business in 1948.

A New Era

Emerging in 1926, the Colored Players' first two films, *A Prince of His Race* and *Ten Nights in a Barroom*, were not much more than standard or slightly updated stories. In 1927, however, it produced *Scar of Shame*, which critics regard as the company's masterpiece. It showed a true struggle among African Americans as they really lived.

Scar of Shame was disturbing to black audiences. It explored the sensitive subject of a rigid class system within the black community, which was difficult to think about. In the film, a light-skinned concert pianist and music teacher named Alvin rescues Louise, a darker-skinned girl who is being beaten by her brutal, drunken stepfather. They fall in love and marry but are ultimately pulled apart by their different positions within the African American social order. Rather than having the lovers triumph over their difficulties, the movie ends with Louise committing suicide and Alvin marrying another lighter-skinned student.

Scar of Shame in 1927, Micheaux's *Wages of Sin* in 1929, and *The Exile* in 1931 were among the last of the silent race movies. Nearly all black producers were independent and could not afford the equipment they needed to make the new and popular sound pictures. Moreover, only a few black theater owners could afford the necessary renovations to allow their theaters to show "talkies," or movies with sound, so the rise in this new film type was yet another obstacle for African Americans to overcome. Micheaux survived in the industry, making movies as late as 1948, but even he was forced into retirement. However, Micheaux and other pioneers, such as the Johnson brothers, had shown that there was an audience for black films, and that black filmmakers could achieve at least a little commercial success.

CHAPTER THREE
STILL SERVING ON SCREEN

Though the early 20th century was a difficult time for African Americans, some intelligent, enterprising, and artistic individuals were making headway in the motion picture industry. *The Birth of a Nation*, though still one of the most racially insensitive blockbuster films ever produced, sparked a backlash from the black community that actually helped put African American filmmakers on the map. Though typecast roles, such as the "tom" and "buck" characters, were still prevalent in mainstream movies, some groundbreaking work was taking place to remove some of Hollywood's racial prejudice.

The rise of "talkies" was initially a setback for racial equality in films. Producers and directors reverted back to creating black characters as racial stereotypes, because that is what many white people expected and wanted to see. The most prominent of those roles was that of a servant. Though the end of the Civil War was nearing its 100-year anniversary, millions of Americans still believed that black people were best suited to serve whites; this was reinforced through film.

As movies with sound became more and more widespread throughout the 1930s and 1940s, the nation was also experiencing a gradual push toward more racial equality. Within the film industry, black stars became well known, some studios broadened the thematic scope of their movies, and African Americans were selected to play a wider variety of roles. Civil rights organizations, politicians, and even white activists demanded these changes. By the time the United States entered World War II, some of the most widespread stereotypes about black people had ended—both in reality and on the big screen.

An Old South State of Mind

In the late 1920s and early 1930s, just as "talkies" started to spread, Hollywood productions depicted African Americans mostly in an Old South context, and that was clearly reflected in early all-black musicals. Two major studios competed to produce the first film in this genre. Director King Vidor, a white Texan, claimed that he was interested in the "sincerity and fervor of [black people's] religious expression … [and] the honest simplicity of their [desires]."[20] He convinced Metro-Goldwyn-Mayer (MGM) to produce a black musical, with him as the director. At the same time, producer William Fox wanted to expand an upcoming short film about life for black people in the post-Civil War South.

Fox made it to the screen first with *Hearts in Dixie* in the spring of 1929. The film starred black actors Clarence Muse as a dignified tenant farmer, Bernice Pilot as his daughter, and Stepin Fetchit in his first major role as the son-in-law with no ambition. Though the movie was essentially a simple drama that had a few scenes of dancing and songs performed by a black choir, it was praised by white critics and hailed by some black writers as a major step forward. The actors agreed. Muse argued that black people

Hearts in Dixie *was the first musical "talkie" with a primarily black cast. It is credited as one of the first major movies to feature Stepin Fetchit.*

needed to take their time integrating into the white-dominated film industry, saying, "This is the game we must build ourselves into."[21]

Other observers were not so sure the film was a success for racial inclusion. Some claimed that the black cast was still being used to fill certain stereotypical roles, even if they were not as extreme as the older "coon" or "mammy" characters of the 1910s.

Critic Henry Dobb wrote, "The tragedy is not the tragedy in the film, but the tragedy of the film; the tragedy of these untainted folk strutting their stuff to the required pattern, playing their parts as the white man likes to believe."[22]

More Musical Theater

King Vidor's musical film was released in August 1929, and it was named *Hallelujah*. It took a harder look at black life in the South, focusing on the stress that families split by migration to the North experienced. Like Fox's *Hearts in Dixie*, *Hallelujah* was well received by critics, although some black writers complained that it went too far in contrasting the simple, moral lifestyle of the South with the wickedness of the North's urban ghetto. They argued that the film implicitly encouraged the Old South lifestyle, which put whites above blacks.

The production company Radio-Keith-Orpheum (RKO) jumped in on this new musical trend later in 1929 with the film *St. Louis Blues*. It featured the great blues singer Bessie Smith in a leading role. However, none of these three early musical films fared as well at the box office as they did with critics. Black films were rare throughout the 1930s, because studios simply could not make very much money producing them. Moreover, many of the nation's most talented singers and dancers were relegated to shorter entertainment films, which were not as widespread as feature-length movies.

Not until 1936 would another major African American film, *The Green Pastures*, be produced. Based on a popular stage play, it retold stories from the biblical Old Testament, as interpreted by children in a black Sunday school. White critical reception was mixed. Among most black critics, responses to the film were openly hostile. The entire film, they argued, was based around a series of stereotypical and inaccurate portrayals of uneducated black interpretations of the Bible. Furthermore, many writers of both races condemned the film as being directly disrespectful to Christianity. Like most of the major African American films that had preceded it, *The Green Pastures* was a commercial disappointment. It did, however, make a star out of Rex Ingram, who played multiple roles in the film, and it was the movie debut of Eddie Anderson, who would later gain fame as comedian Jack Benny's sidekick, a personal servant named Rochester.

WALKING A FINE LINE

Critical reception was mixed for *The Green Pastures*. Some critics thought the film was charming, while others considered it disrespectful of Christianity. Some found its portrayal of blacks to be quaint, but others saw it as condescending. Critic Margaret Farrand Thorp understood both points of view:

> The producer [Jack Warner] is ready to protect the Negro and avoid stirring race hatreds by keeping off the modern screen such villainous Negroes as appeared in Griffith's "The Birth of a Nation," but the best he thinks he can do beyond that is to make the Negro so amusing and agreeable that an audience is always pleased at the appearance of a black face ... The all-Negro "The Green Pastures," for all its originality and, at some points, elevation, permitted, however, a certain feeling of superiority on the part of the [white] audience.[1]

1. Quoted in Peter Noble, *The Negro in Films*. New York, NY: Arno, 1970, p. 9.

Servants and Stereotypes

It is noteworthy that Anderson was best known for playing the role of servant to a white man. For most black actors in the 1930s, that was the role they were stuck with. As Donald Bogle wrote, "No other period in motion-picture history could boast of more black faces carrying mops and pails or lifting pots and pans than the [1930s]."[23] Some African American intellectuals criticized actors for accepting such demeaning parts, but the actors defended themselves, saying that though their roles were not glamorous, they emphasized some admirable traits. Louise Beavers, for example, famous for her roles as a meek, polite maid, said she wanted "my public to know me as playing these loving character parts."[24]

There was not much to admire, however, in the traits frequently portrayed by actor Stepin Fetchit, another major African American actor of the time. He made more than 50 films in his career, and most of the time, he played the same character: a slow-moving,

Though Stepin Fetchit experienced widespread fame and was featured in many films, the roles he played were rarely flattering. Many critics have accused him of playing into black stereotypes.

stereotype was popular with most white audiences, particularly when Fetchit teamed up with white comedian Will Rogers. Millions of white moviegoers laughed at his antics, but most black people believed that the role was demeaning and degrading for African Americans all across the country.

Different Actors, Same Stereotypes

Despite outrage from black critics, Fetchit's success led Hollywood to cast other African American actors to play the same undignified role. Many actors even embraced the stereotype. Willie Best, early in his film career, went by the name "Sleep 'n' Eat," a play on the racist claim that all a black man needed to keep him happy was a place to sleep and enough to eat. Mantan Moreland, another black actor, was frequently cast as a sidekick to a highly intellectual character, such as detective Charlie Chan, and would tremble with fear and run at the first sign of danger.

dim-witted, head-scratching buffoon. In this role, he exasperated his white masters, to whom he was nonetheless an overly respectful servant. These roles are common examples of the "coon" character type, which is considered to be one of the most offensive stereotypes among African Americans. As such, black critics spoke out against Fetchit's commonly-played character type. However, the "coon"

Two of Fetchit's successors were unique because their acting was secondary to other talents: music in the case of Louis Armstrong and dance in the case of Bill "Bojangles" Robinson. Although black musicians were often included in Hollywood movies as nightclub performers apart from the main plot, jazz trumpeter Armstrong

Louis Armstrong was one of the most famous musicians of the 1920s and 1930s. His fame and skill with a trumpet even landed him some minor speaking parts in major Hollywood productions.

was famous enough that he frequently had speaking roles. Even with a minor speaking part, his characters were generally similar to other African American stereotyped characters—he was often clueless and easily confused.

Robinson, a highly renowned dancer, reached the height of his movie fame in four films where he starred alongside the extremely popular Shirley Temple. The most successful of these movies were *The Little Colonel* and *The Littlest Rebel*, both

released in 1935. The films returned to a Civil War time period, portraying Robinson as the faithful family servant who becomes a guardian and protector of Temple's character.

Though Robinson's films with Temple were widely successful, many observers pointed out the tension between having black males paired with white females, which had been in the public subconscious since *The Birth of a Nation*. No one objected to Robinson, the good servant, dancing with little Shirley. However, when Armstrong was partnered with white singer Martha Raye (who wore blackface in the performance) in a musical number, it drew widespread protest and censorship.

Changing Views of Sidekicks

It was Eddie "Rochester" Anderson who took the black male sidekick role in a new direction in the mid-1930s. Wisecracking and back-talking in his trademark gravelly voice, Rochester frequently outwitted Jack Benny, his white costar, and never hesitated to point out his boss's shortcomings. He may have been a servant to Benny, but he was rarely explicitly inferior to him.

By the time Anderson had perfected his back-talking character in the late 1930s, black female servants in movies had been playing a similar role for years. The decade had not started out that way, however. Popular white actresses, such as Mae West and Jean Harlow, generally played glamorous characters attended by African American maids with stereotypically black names, such as Beulah, Petunia, or Jemima. The white women sometimes confided in their maids, but there was no equality between them.

Louise Beavers, a black actress, excelled in such roles, which led to her most important film: 1934's *Imitation of Life*. Beavers played Delilah, a woman who is taken in as a housekeeper by a white widow named Bea. Soon, the pair are running a home-based pancake flour business and raising their daughters. The business and the girls grow and thrive over several years. Delilah primarily remains meek and subservient; when the now-wealthy Bea tells her partner that she can afford to buy her own house, Delilah protests that she just wants to remain a cook for Bea. She claims that all she wants is a simple life, ending with an extravagant funeral.

Much of the drama of the plot revolves around Delilah's relationship with her light-skinned daughter, Peola, who is ashamed of being black and tries to pass as white. This was a highly sensitive issue, and *Imitation of Life* was one of the first major Hollywood films to address it. When she is accidentally exposed by her mother, Peola speaks out against the racial injustice in America. The submissive Delilah, however, tells her to "Open up and say, 'Lord, I bows my head.'"[25] Many viewers criticized the character of Delilah, and the movie is often cited as an example of segregation-era films that show black people eagerly adopting the values of white culture. Though Delilah's character was poorly reviewed, Beavers's performance was exceptional, and many critics thought she should have been nominated for an Academy Award.

McDaniel and "Mammies"

A change came only a year later when Hattie McDaniel played Katherine Hepburn's maid in 1935's *Alice Adams*. She did not fulfill the stereotypical "mammy" role that most African American maids did in films. McDaniel's trademark persona—a strong, outspoken, no-nonsense black woman—had emerged when she played Stepin Fetchit's wife in *Judge Priest*, a 1934 comedy. In *Alice Adams*, her bold speech is directed not at her black husband, but at her white mistress. Her strong opinions are obvious, even when she expresses

Hattie McDaniel, whose most famous role was Mammy in Gone with the Wind, *revolutionized the stereotypical black maid character. She was bold, strong, and unintimidated by white society.*

In these performances, however, McDaniel was just warming up for her signature role. In 1939's *Gone with the Wind*, she was cast in the signature role of black women in the 1930s, widely considered the ultimate servant portrayal: a maid actually named Mammy. Black characters were a central part of the plot of Margaret Mitchell's wildly popular Civil War-era novel, on which the movie was based, and producer David Selznick was determined that African Americans "come out decidedly on the [positive] side of the ledger"[26] in the film version.

After the film came out, McDaniel came to be closely identified with Mammy. *Gone with the Wind* won the Academy Award for Best Picture, and Hattie McDaniel was the first African American to be awarded an Oscar for Best Supporting Actress. She was also the first black woman to attend the award ceremony as a nominee instead of servant.

herself only with a disdainful grunt or an unhappy glare. Her character was unique and individualistic—revolutionary in 1935.

In *The Mad Miss Manton*, produced in 1938, McDaniel keeps her society girl mistress, played by Barbara Stanwyck, in line with her assertive comments. In some instances, McDaniel's character directly and aggressively talks back to her white employer. The actress had further refined the role of an outspoken maid, and she was reinventing the "mammy" character that many black women had to play.

"FOUL SLANDER AGAINST THE NEGRO PEOPLE"

Much like *The Birth of a Nation*, *Gone with the Wind* was an immediate and spectacular success. It is included on many lists of the best films ever made. Also like its predecessor, however, *Gone with the Wind* was criticized for its portrayal of blacks. One of the strongest statements against the movie came from the New York office of the American Communist Party:

Gone with the Wind *revives every foul slander against the Negro people, every ... lie [told by] the Southern lynchers. While dressed in a slick package of sentimentality for the old "noble" traditions of the South, this movie is a rabid [insult to] the Negro people. The historical struggle for democracy in this country which we have come to cherish so dearly is vilified and condemned ... Not only is this vicious picture calculated to provoke race riots, but also to cause sectional strife between the North and the South just when the growth of the labor and progressive movement has made possible the increasing unity of Negro and white, in behalf of the common interest of both.*[1]

1. Quoted in M. Carmen Gómez-Galisteo, *The Wind Is Never Gone: Sequels, Parodies and Rewritings of* Gone with the Wind. Jefferson, NC: McFarland & Company, 2011, p. 59.

Maid and Mistress

When Selznick saw what McDaniel could bring to the role, it was obvious that she should play Mammy. Mammy's character is a maid to Scarlett O'Hara, the spoiled, rich, white heroine. She is also a mother figure; she advises, scolds, or comforts Scarlett, as the situation requires. She is both physically and emotionally protective of her mistress. Mammy has an ability to see through people's lies, and she is quick to call people on their foolishness.

McDaniel's Mammy was the strongest, boldest, and most sympathetic black character in any film up to that time. She embodied both the no-nonsense humor that had made McDaniel famous and a dramatic intensity that drew praise from critics and won the hearts of audiences. Black leaders, however, had reservations about *Gone with the Wind*. They were eager to praise McDaniel, who was able to play a strong character, but could hardly overlook the way the film treated most African Americans.

In contrast to the dignified Mammy, there was the hysterical, good-for-nothing "pickaninny" character Prissy; the servile Pork; and the clownish Uncle Peter. Most black critics agreed with the observations written in the *Pittsburgh Courier*'s review, which praised the film's artistry and McDaniel's performance, but complained, "much of it was distasteful to the Negro race."[27] When McDaniel was awarded the Oscar for Best Supporting Actress, however, many African American observers were pleased. She was a groundbreaker for black actors and motion picture professionals.

Setting New Standards

Although servants made up the bulk of major black roles in the 1930s, there were a few significant exceptions. In 1933's *The Emperor Jones*, Paul Robeson plays a former railroad porter who escapes from jail to a Caribbean island, where he eventually becomes an "emperor" who issues orders to his white former partner. "Black audiences must have felt immensely proud," one historian wrote, to see Robeson "telling them white folks to get outta his way."[28]

Several films dealt with the controversial subject of lynching in the 1930s. Two, however—*Fury* in 1936 and *They Won't Forget* in 1937—concentrated on mob violence instead of racial tensions. Also produced in 1937, *Black Legion* was more to the point and was a surprisingly bold attack, for Hollywood's standards, on the Ku Klux Klan and other racist organizations.

A handful of movies dealt with blacks not as servants, but as criminals. *Bullets or Ballots* in 1936 showed Louise Beavers break away from her "mammy" roles to play the leader of an inner-city gambling ring. Edward Thompson was a hip, wisecracking African American gunman in *The Petrified Forest* in 1936. This character was a forerunner of the street-smart black film heroes that would appear in the 1970s.

At the other end of the social scale, Clarence Brooks played a dignified, dedicated doctor in 1931's *Arrowsmith*. This probably marked the first time a mainstream movie showed an African American as an educated professional.

A More Equal Time

Though films similar to *Arrowsmith* were certainly far from common, African Americans made significant progress in the film industry in 1930s. Many black actors were still playing servants at the end of the decade, but Hattie McDaniel's bold Mammy in 1939 was quite different from Louise Beavers's meek Delilah in 1934. Though Stepin Fetchit's role as Joe in 1929's *Show Boat* was demeaning, Paul Robeson brought strong dignity to the same role in *Show Boat*'s 1936 remake.

The United States was approaching a time of dramatic change in the 1940s. World War II was on the horizon, and with it came a need for citizens to unite in the face of a common enemy. In 1942, Walter White, executive secretary of the NAACP, issued a statement that called on Hollywood to ensure that the "picturization of the Negro [no longer be] as comic or [unimportant] figures but as normal human beings."[29] This would not be an easy task to accomplish.

CHAPTER FOUR
THE FILM INDUSTRY AND WORLD WAR II

Though there were still plenty of films being released that only allowed black actors to play stereotypical roles, a newer brand of cinema was being created in the early 1940s. Strong and talented black actors in the late 1930s had paved the way for a wider variety of roles for African Americans. Even some of the stereotyped characters, such as "mammy," were being revolutionized, which made them less discriminatory toward black people and black culture. Wartime movies continued this trend.

When the United States entered into World War II in 1941, the national economy was stimulated, America grew into a world superpower, and there was greater acceptance of racial equality. There are a number of reasons for this. Activist groups, such as the NAACP, had successfully campaigned for more people to view African American individuals as equal to whites. Politicians

realized that they needed black support to get elected. Perhaps most importantly, however, the nation realized that it needed to remove some of the divisions between races if it was going to win the war. One of the most important social developments happened through Hollywood's numerous wartime films.

Not only was the film industry enlisted to create propaganda movies, which were meant to generate optimism and confidence in America, but it also found profitability in addressing broad social issues in the 1940s. Black and white Americans served side by side in the armed forces, so more people were willing to accept greater racial equality. One of the first films to demonstrate this was *In This Our Life*, released in 1942, in which Ernest Anderson played an intelligent black youth unjustly accused of a hit-and-run. His character maintains his poise and integrity until the real culprit

A STRONG MEDIUM

The power of motion pictures to shape people's attitudes was immense. Even in the 1940s, movies were a way of showing people things they had never seen—and of reinforcing stereotypes. Historian Lawrence Reddick wrote about how racism was spread through movies:

> Directly and indirectly [the film industry] establishes associations and drives deeper into the public mind the stereotyped conception of the Negro. By building up this unfavorable conception, the movies operate to [prevent] the advancement of the Negro, to humiliate him, to weaken his drive for equality, and to spread indifference, contempt, and hatred for him and his cause. This great agency for the communication of ideas and information, therefore, functions as a powerful instrument for maintaining the racial subordination of the Negro people.[1]

1. Quoted in Anna Everett, *Returning the Gaze: A Genealogy of Black Film Criticism, 1909–1949*. Durham, NC: Duke University Press, 2001, p. 288.

confesses. The *New York Times* praised the film for its "brief but frank allusion to racial discrimination."[30]

Global Issues

The United States was a new combatant in World War II when *In This Our Life* came out, and international politics had raised Americans' awareness of racial discrimination. The treatment of Jews in Germany and in occupied European countries under Adolf Hitler's Nazi regime had demonstrated the extremes to which racism could be taken. The persecution of European Jews made Americans uncomfortably aware of the historical suffering of black people in their own country.

As the United States fought in the war, a national sense of urgency and the need for unity intensified. The war called for unprecedented military and manufacturing commitments. The country needed African Americans to participate more than ever before. Black leaders saw this as a clear opportunity to achieve what some black activists called the "Double V"—victory over enemies overseas and victory over racism at

The Nazi regime in Germany used posters such as this to stir up hatred for Jewish people. Many white Americans began to have more of a social conscience about their own treatment of African Americans as the horrors of the Nazis were exposed.

home. Walter White declared that blacks would "fight for liberties here while waging war against dictators abroad."[31] The struggle for black Americans, wrote Cripps, was to find a way for "short-run national necessity [to] be shaped into a long-run politics of civil rights."[32]

Activism at Work

Ever since *The Birth of a Nation* came out in 1915, the NAACP had been trying to get Hollywood to give black people more meaningful roles and to show them, White said, "as ... normal human being[s] and integral part[s] of human life and activity."[33] For the NAACP, this meant depicting blacks as members of an integrated society, taking their places alongside whites in schools, churches, the workplace, and other routine activities of everyday life.

Fortunately, White had the federal government as an ally. Politicians knew that the country would need large numbers of black and white people in the armed forces and on factory assembly lines. Some officials were worried that black Americans might be susceptible to enemy propaganda, telling them this was a white man's war in which they had no stake. To fight this, President Franklin D. Roosevelt realized that the government needed an organized effort to convey the message of unity and equality.

In June 1942, he created the Office of War Information (OWI), which he tasked with producing newsreels and overseeing the content of motion pictures. The OWI pressured Hollywood to not only include more black roles, but also to see that such roles did not merely fulfill derogatory

BREAKING OUT OF RACE ROLES

The NAACP had long been concerned with how African Americans were depicted in films. Of particular concern was the issue of black actors who agreed to play stereotypical and demeaning roles. In 1942, NAACP executive secretary Walter White issued what he called a "statement to the Negro public, particularly in Los Angeles":

Walter White was an outspoken activist devoted to the cause of African American rights. He called for more equality in the film industry.

Our utmost wisdom and intelligence must be used by Negro actors, present and future, and by the Negro public generally on the pledges which have been made by the motion picture industry to broaden the treatment of the Negro in films ... [there need to be] more acting roles for Negroes in motion pictures [and more] employment of qualified colored men and women in the technical end of the production.

As for those actors in Hollywood who can play only comic or servant roles, I trust they will not let their own interests spoil the opportunity we now have to correct a lot of things from which Negroes have suffered in the past in the movies.[1]

1. Quoted in Thomas Cripps, *Slow Fade to Black*. New York, NY: Oxford University Press, 1993, p. 387.

stereotypes. Although the OWI did not admit any intent to solve the country's racial problems, it was nevertheless, according to a staff manual, "particularly interested in all appearances of dark-skinned races."[34]

Industry Insiders

Outside of Washington, D.C., White also had allies in Hollywood. Darryl Zanuck, a producer at 20th Century Fox, and independent producer Walter Wanger were genuinely sympathetic to

White's cause. Some big-name stars, such as Humphrey Bogart and John Garfield, and prominent directors, such as Mervyn LeRoy and Frank Capra, also supported a more diverse industry.

Not everyone was as willing to accept change, though, and the NAACP had some enemies as well. Conservative politicians in Congress, primarily southern men, accused some of White's Hollywood sympathizers of having associations with the Communist Party. Anti-Communist beliefs were used to discredit progressive thinkers. Moreover, some major producers, such as Frank Freeman at Paramount Pictures, did not like what they considered outside interference in the industry.

Ironically, a lot of the opposition came from established black actors, such as Willie Best, Hattie McDaniel, and Eddie Anderson. Their livelihoods depended on the kind of roles that White wanted to eliminate from film. Anderson would later dismiss White as "an Eastern phoney trying to be white."[35] This was a significant and degrading insult.

Despite some protests from powerful voices, the servant roles almost disappeared during the 1940s. Wartime pictures tended to avoid portraying rich whites with black maids and butlers. Some traditional roles, however, still made it onto the screen. Best played his typical role as an incompetent fool in *The Kansan* in 1943, and McDaniel was once more a maid in *Since You Went Away* the following year.

A New Era of Musicals

After the relatively unsuccessful early black musical films, few had been produced during the 1930s. Paul Robeson, who had been largely inactive in the late 1930s, was convinced to star in the black segment of *Tales of Manhattan* in 1942. The film had scenes of happy, smiling black people singing and dancing in the cotton fields. This drew widespread ridicule, because it appeared to glorify slavery. Robeson himself said, "I wouldn't blame any Negro for picketing this film."[36]

Cabin in the Sky received a similar reception when it was released the following year. This film placed black people in a fantasy world, similar to 1936's *The Green Pastures*. It starred Eddie Anderson as a gambler whose soul is the subject of a duel between heaven and hell. Despite praise for the performances of Anderson, Ethel Waters, Lena Horne, Rex Ingram, and other African American stars, *TIME* magazine dismissed their characters as "picturesque, [stereotypical] entertainers."[37]

The other all-black musical of 1943 was the very different film titled *Stormy Weather*. Featuring Horne and Bill "Bojangles" Robinson, the film portrayed the history of black entertainers over the previous 25 years. Even though it avoided some of the stereotypes of *Cabin in the Sky*, some critics have noted that it "[portrayed] African America as a happy place with happy problems."[38] Its modern theme and jazzy music, however, had a wide appeal for audiences.

An Adapted Role

The goal of the NAACP and the OWI, however, was not to produce more black films. What they really wanted was to see blacks in meaningful roles alongside whites. To create these new positions, however, Hollywood needed to abandon most of the traditional servant and sidekick roles that black actors played. To make a new place for African American actors, Hollywood adapted a stock character from the western film genre—the loner who lived apart from society. In westerns, that character could be the mysterious gunman who comes to the aid of peaceful townspeople; a black actor taking this new protagonist role would interact with a small number of whites and, in the process, enrich their lives. This theme, wrote one film expert, "would define a black place in American life for the next generation."[39]

World War II provided the ideal dramatic setting for such a theme. The most prominent cinematic examples were *Sahara*, *Crash Dive*, and *Bataan*, all released in 1943, and *Lifeboat*, which came out the following year. All these films featured black characters whose bravery and integrity were important

Bill "Bojangles" Robinson was famous for his incredible talent as a dancer. Later in his career, however, he moved to other forms of entertainment, including acting. His movie Stormy Weather *was especially popular, even if it was not especially groundbreaking.*

AMERICAN UNITY

To support the war effort, the United States was forced into a huge amount of manufacturing and, along with it, a massive need for labor. Many jobs from which blacks had traditionally been forbidden were now open to them. The government wanted all Americans to feel that they were part of the war effort, regardless of their race, and one of the methods considered important was to portray ethnic minorities in a more positive light than in the past.

The governmental body that oversaw the depiction of minorities in motion pictures and other forms of entertainment was the Office of War Information. The work of the OWI and its importance was described in a 1943 *New York Times* article:

[T]wo major studios, Metro-Goldwyn-Mayer and Twentieth Century-Fox, in producing pictures with all-Negro casts, are following the desires of Washington in making such films at this time. Decisions to produce the pictures, it is stated, followed official expression that the [presidential] Administration felt that its program for increased employment of Negro citizens in certain [typically] restricted fields of industry would be helped by a general distribution of important pictures in which Negroes played a major part.[1]

1. Quoted in Donald Bogle, *Toms, Coons, Mulattoes, Mammies & Bucks: An Interpretive History of Blacks in American Film.* New York, NY: Continuum, 2006, p. 137.

contributions to the story line.

Sahara was different from the others because its main black character was not an American, but a soldier from Sudan, played by Rex Ingram, who joins an American tank crew and other Allied soldiers lost in the North African desert. The white characters in *Sahara* look to the black character for guidance across the desert, and he is ultimately killed trying to save his new friends. This was a bold new role for a black actor, and the movie received positive reviews.

A Race of Heroes

In both *Crash Dive* and *Lifeboat*, however, black actors play Americans who are not equal in status with the white characters. *Crash Dive* features a character based on the real-life Dorie Miller, a cook on an American battleship who manned a machine gun during the attack on Pearl Harbor and shot down at least one Japanese plane. In *Lifeboat*, a small group of survivors adrift on the ocean includes an African American steward named Joe, who saved one of the women from drowning. When some of the others team up to kill a German sailor, Joe refuses, having once witnessed a lynching. Both of these characters were heroic, even if they were not equal to their white counterparts.

Bataan put its black main character on a more even footing with whites than the others. Wesley, played by actor Kenneth Spencer, is a former minister who has been trained in the army as a demolitions expert and is part of a patrol lost in the Philippines. He offers a prayer over the grave of a fallen comrade and is killed with the rest of the soldiers. A *New York Times* reviewer wrote, "Kenneth Spencer has quiet strength and simple dignity as a Negro soldier from the engineers—a character whose placement in the picture is one of the outstanding merits of it."[40]

The black characters in these films, even though they were unquestionably heroic, portrayed black people in a white world where they were simply not as important. Blacks and whites could be forced together by wartime necessity in a boat or on a military patrol, but they could not live, work, or attend school together in the same neighborhood. "No one," wrote one film historian, "imagined any other arrangement, at least for now."[41]

Unity and Communism

When the war ended in 1945, it became more difficult to find popular situations where the black loner role could easily fit in. The dominant theme of films was no longer national unity, but adjusting to peacetime. Most of white America was concerned with the experience of white, not black, veterans who were returning home from the war. In fact, one film dealing with the subject, *Till the End of Time*, released in 1946, changed all the characters from the original book from black to white.

Walter White and the NAACP also began to lose their influence in Hollywood. The OWI's motion picture office closed in 1944, brought on by pressure from conservative congressmen and the end of the war. White proposed the establishment of a permanent NAACP film agency, but the idea did not get an encouraging reception from anyone in Hollywood, even White's closest allies.

Indeed, the end of the war brought a dramatic decrease in the more positive black roles that had emerged in the early 1940s. In their place, there was a return to conservative, traditional, and racist portrayals. Producers were more concerned with profits and tended to avoid anything controversial, especially as the House Un-American Activities Committee (HUAC) began investigating alleged Communists in the film industry. Harry Cohn, an executive at Columbia Pictures, summed up the mood in Hollywood when he said, "Give me somethin' I can use and nothing controversial—like [black people] or God."[42]

During the years immediately following the end of World War II, many unique and bold film ideas were never produced. The threat of Nazi Germany had been replaced, in many people's opinion, by the threat of Communist Russia. After years of fighting and a new threat from Europe, most of white America wanted simple entertainment. As a result, black actors were forced back into the stereotypical and racially insensitive roles of the 1930s.

Safe Black Roles

The best example of what was considered a "safe black role," which generally meant a stereotyped character, was that of Uncle Remus in Disney's 1946 *Song of the South*. Based on the Joel Chandler Harris stories, the film featured Uncle Remus telling white children tales of Br'er Rabbit, Br'er Fox, and Br'er Bear, all of which were animated figures.

Song of the South embodied basically everything the NAACP had been fighting against for decades. The organization said that the movie gave "an impression of [a pleasant] master-slave relationship which is a distortion of the fact."[43] The *New York Times* criticized the producer for "putting out such a story in this troubled day and age."[44] That same article accused Walt Disney of, similarly to D.W. Griffith, glorifying the Old South.

This image from Song of the South *shows Uncle Remus with a child from the movie. The Remus character drew widespread criticism for enforcing outdated and racist stereotypes.*

White audiences, however, loved the film and praised James Baskett, the veteran vaudeville actor who played the role of Remus after other black stars had turned it down. Even some black critics, such as the NAACP's Gloster Current, while harshly denouncing the movie, agreed that Baskett was "artistic and dynamic."[45] As it had been with Hattie McDaniel, criticism of Baskett was quieted when he received an Honorary Academy Award for his performance.

Despite these significant setbacks, African American groups still fought for more equality in film. The modest success of wartime documentaries, such as *The Negro Soldier* and *Teamwork* in 1944, led to similar postwar efforts to highlight racial issues across the country. Although such films as *To Secure These Rights*, *The Color of Man*, and *The Quiet One* were rarely seen in theaters, they found audiences in union halls, schools, and public libraries.

Motion Pictures with a Message

Many documentaries such as these were praised by film critics and by activist organizations, even if the public was largely unaware of them. This may be one reason Hollywood started to risk controversial subject matter once again, and an eruption of "message" films followed—*Home of the Brave*, *Lost Boundaries*, *Pinky*, and *Intruder in the Dust* were all released in 1949. These films, Cripps wrote, "signaled the opening of an era warmed by a sense of urgency [and] also a sense that the four years of maturing since the war placed them on the verge of the most important peacetime era of race relations since Reconstruction."[46]

The way toward equality for African Americans had been partially cleared by the success of two films dealing with anti-Semitism (discrimination against Jews)—*Gentleman's Agreement* and *Crossfire* in 1947—and by the film *Body and Soul*, also released in 1947, in which a black former boxer played an important role. *Home of the Brave*, one of the first of the message films, is remarkable because the primary character was deliberately rewritten from a Jewish man to a black man by the studio. It contains some of the most forceful language ever heard from a black character in a movie. Peter Moss, the black main character, says to a white character, "I learned that if you're colored, you stink. You're not like other people. You're—you're alone. You're something strange, different ... Well, you make us different, you rats."[47]

Lost Boundaries revisited the theme of black people wanting to pass as white people. When a couple's true ethnicity is revealed to their New England neighbors, their children struggle under the burden. *Pinky* echoed the same theme, and Ethel Waters's performance as one of the black main characters earned her an Academy Award nomination. Both films, however, cast white actors, such as Mel Ferrer and Jeanne Crain, to play black roles. This reflected both the studios' caution and their reliance on stars who would attract white audiences.

A New Kind of Character

Intruder in the Dust examined the subject of lynching in a new way. The character of Lucas Beauchamp was played by Juano Hernandez, who was of Puerto Rican and African descent. Beauchamp is not the meek, calm, unjustly accused black victim, which was a common theme in past films. Instead, he is proud and arrogant, dressed in suit and tie with a gold toothpick in his mouth, walking confidently into a Mississippi general store under the hateful gaze of whites. Although he is ultimately cleared of the charge of murder, he never begs or pleads, as many black characters in movies used to do. Rather, he treats his captors with a quiet contempt. At the end of the film, some of the white characters realize that they almost lynched an innocent man due to their racism. This was a powerful message at the time.

The 1950s opened with *No Way Out*, the film that launched black actor Sidney Poitier to stardom as he played a young doctor who must treat a pair of wounded, racist criminals. Even when he is shot by one of them, he saves the man's life. His character is complex and intellectual. *No Way Out* was also noteworthy because it provided a breakout role for Ruby Dee, who would costar with Poitier in some of the decade's most important films.

In the space of 11 years, Hollywood had gone from Hattie McDaniel's strong-willed Mammy to Sidney Poitier's thoughtful Dr. Brooks, and the entire United States had undergone an equally dramatic change. World War II had created a sense of unity and an awareness of the inequality that undermined that unity. Though a few years after the war's end saw Hollywood revert back to racist stereotypes, by 1949, black actors were being given important roles. Motion pictures had done a lot to expose the problem of racial discrimination, and they would do even more in the decade to come.

CHAPTER FIVE
CIVIL RIGHTS AND HOLLYWOOD PROFITS

African Americans in film had undergone a series of transformations during the 1940s. World War II initially brought black and white people together, and this was reflected on the big screen. After the end of the war, however, many white studios believed it would be more profitable to return to the racial stereotypes of years past. Then, as the 1950s approached, some studios began reinventing the image of black characters in American film.

The increase in prominent black roles in 1950s films coincided with the rise of the American civil rights movement. Beginning in the middle of the decade, millions of dissatisfied black citizens were organizing peaceful protests all across the country, demanding to be heard. As politicians were slow to adopt many racial changes, some aggravated activists began to protest through violence.

Hollywood, during this time, most-ly followed the prevalent national mood. As an industry, its primary concern was with profits, and the way they made money was by getting as many people as possible to the theater. In the early years of the civil rights movement, America's national mood was undecided about whether it would follow the path of racial equality or the path of continued racial oppression. Film companies knew that pushing too hard for equality would lead to a decreased customer base. Furthermore, the HUAC was investigating anyone in Hollywood who was being too progressive. Taking a risk in filmmaking during this time would likely lead to being blacklisted, or denied work in the industry. As a result, major motion picture studios reverted back to the simplest thing to both draw in audiences and keep their jobs: stereotyping black people.

Just for Show

There were plenty of films with black characters in the 1950s, but few movies that advocated for black people. Hollywood thought it sufficient, Cripps wrote, to "[limit] racial discourse to the admission of a single iconic black into a white [group]."[48] In later years, this would be known as tokenism, and the single black character in a film full of white people would be called a "token black."

Nevertheless, during the 1950s, several black actors reached a level of unprecedented stardom. Their films, for the most part, were uncontroversial, and although black critics might have complained, the new middle-class black audiences embraced them, as did many white viewers.

Black actors had played strong characters before, but few had been so central to a major Hollywood film as Ethel Waters in *The Member of the Wedding*, released in 1952. As the housekeeper Berenice, she comforts, advises, and protects two white children. She is a "mammy" figure, but unlike Hattie McDaniel's characters, she is strong and gentle without making either characteristic over-the-top. She is nevertheless a traditional "mammy," and this role echoed the past instead of signaling the future.

Weak Films

The first big all-black production of the decade was titled *Carmen Jones*. Produced in 1954, it was a film version of a Broadway musical. Although it featured established stars, including singers Pearl Bailey and Harry Belafonte, Dorothy Dandridge dominated the film in the title role. Her performance made her the first black woman to earn an Academy Award nomination for Best Actress.

The film itself, however, had nothing to do with black issues. The plot primarily involved a love triangle that was not unique or related to African American life. Racial attitudes were visible, however, because there was little physical intimacy in this version of the love story. Physical intimacy between blacks was all but prohibited in Hollywood ever since *The Birth of a Nation* in 1915.

This policy was especially evident in 1957's *Island in the Sun*. The original story, a novel by Alec Waugh, had examined racial tensions on a Caribbean island, and it included love affairs between a black man and white woman and between a black woman and white man. The production of *Island in the Sun*, however, began during a landmark civil rights event in the United States: the Montgomery, Alabama, bus boycott led by the Reverend Martin Luther

This image is from Island in the Sun, *a film adaptation of a novel that examined race relations. The movie, however, removed the potentially controversial love scenes between black and white characters.*

King Jr. Though producer Darryl Zanuck had made pro-African American films in the past, he decided to tone down this movie's interracial story line. One prominent character, a militant lawyer, was eliminated altogether, and the love scenes between Dandridge and white actor John Justin, and between Belafonte and white actress Joan Fontaine, were nothing like the book. After the film was released, Dandridge described just how difficult it was to film a romantic scene under Zanuck by saying, "We had to fight to say the word love."[49]

Belafonte and Poitier, two of the major black male stars of the 1950s, both suffered from Hollywood's restrained attitudes. This was especially true in Belafonte's case, because he was extremely talented at singing and not as successful as a traditional actor. *Odds Against Tomorrow*, a film coproduced in 1959 by Belafonte himself, was the only 1950s movie in which he was able to emerge as a multidimensional character. In it, he played a musician down on his luck who joins up with a gang of bank robbers. When the robbery fails, their fragile partnership is torn apart by racism. The message, which was bold in the 1950s, was that racism could similarly tear the country apart.

A Symbol of Friendship

Though the 1950s were not a great time for African Americans in film, Sidney Poitier emerged as the most popular black actor of the decade. After *No Way Out*, he played some supporting roles before scoring big again in *The Blackboard Jungle* in 1955. One of the more honest and hard-hitting films of the 1950s, it examined growing unrest and violence among urban youth. Poitier's character, a student, joins others in mocking a white teacher. By the end of the film, however, he chooses to defend the teacher when a classmate attacks him. This was a relatively dynamic and complex role, especially for an African American character.

The role was also a departure for Poitier himself. Up to that point, he had mostly played calm, restrained, even-tempered characters. In *The*

Sidney Poitier played a number of different roles throughout the mid-1900s. From escaped prisoner to calm doctor, he became known for infusing his characters with life. He is known for starring in movies that encouraged racial cooperation.

Blackboard Jungle, he lashes out against an unjust system and defiantly refuses give in to it. In the end, however, his inherent goodness is what determines his actions. That goodness and intelligence would mark most of Poitier's roles for the rest of his career.

After starring in some bold films and playing powerful leading roles, Poitier was becoming a symbol for American brotherhood, regardless of race. Not only was he extremely well-spoken, but his roles also allowed Poitier to show his acting talents. Two of his 1950s films, *Edge of the City* in 1957 and *The Defiant Ones* in 1958, helped solidify his image as a racial peacemaker. The central plot line of both was the same: black and white men must work together to succeed.

In *Edge of the City*, Poitier is a railroad worker who befriends and gets a job for a white homeless man he finds in a train. Later, he defends his new friend in a fight, and he is killed. Though the film does fall in to some stereotyping, such as a black man dying for a white man, it more prominently highlights that these two men were able to form a friendship. In *The Defiant Ones*, the black man and white man are bound together literally—they are prison escapees, chained together. They develop a friendship across racial boundaries, and Poitier's character sacrifices his freedom to save his white co-star's character. The clearest message in the film is that men of different races can—and need to—cooperate with one another.

Going Nowhere Fast

Sidney Poitier was nominated for an Academy Award for his performance in *The Defiant Ones*, but many black critics did not like his willingness to play a character who sacrifices himself for a white man. The 1950s were coming to an end, and the promises of equality through integration had not been fulfilled. The national debate on race relations was increasingly tense, but Hollywood was slow to reflect these changing attitudes. As the 1960s began, "safe" films were the norm.

Flaming Star, produced in 1960, made one of the strongest statements about racism, but it dealt with Native Americans rather than blacks. In this time period, Hollywood also released a few feature films about the trials of light-skinned black women, but these characters were often played by white actresses, just as in the 1940s. To go along with the increasing integration of professional sports, some celebrated black athletes, such as baseball player Jackie Robinson, tennis star Althea Gibson, boxer Jersey Joe Walcott, and football player Woody Strode, tried their hand at acting. None of their films carried a strong message about racism, and Gibson, far from going against stereotypes, played a traditional maid. To many critics and observers, it appeared that Hollywood "was scared ... to try a really black picture."[50]

There were some good, well-intentioned attempts at realism, one of which was 1961's *A Raisin in the Sun*, which was the only major film that "dared to portray a genuine core of black culture."[51] The cast was primarily black, and it focused on issues facing African Americans. Poitier, in another departure from his cool, calm image, plays a frustrated limousine driver who believes that his work is demeaning and wasteful. He eventually exclaims, "That ain't no kind of a job ... that ain't nothing at all."[52]

A Raisin in the Sun tried to capture and portray the hopelessness and bottled-up frustration of poor urban African Americans, who desperately wanted to escape the ghetto but could not see a way out. In a way that no film before it had accomplished, it examined the pressure and struggles that many black families experienced.

Outside of Hollywood

Most films that were more sensitive to the racial issues of the late 1950s and early 1960s came from independent

SUCCESS ON STAGE AND SCREEN

When Lorraine Hansberry's play, *A Raisin in the Sun*, opened on Broadway early in 1959, producer David Susskind immediately began working to secure the rights to make a movie based on it. He wrote to an executive at Columbia Pictures that he would be able to acquire the movie rights because he knew Hansberry. He was interested in making the play into a film because, he wrote, the play was "a profoundly moving story of [N]egro life in which ... the race issue is not paramount."[1]

David Susskind received immediate critical renown for 1961's A Raisin in the Sun. *He was not afraid of addressing the troubling issues of racism and the lives of poor African Americans in the 1950s.*

After the film was released, Susskind received good reviews and several letters of praise from industry leaders. One, from a television executive, read, "Perhaps more in this industry than any other we are judged by what we do when we have the opportunity to do it ... You and your associates have produced an even more immediate and compelling piece than the play itself. It is indeed a credit to the movie industry."[2]

1. Quoted in Mark A. Reid, *Redefining Black Film*. Los Angeles, CA: University of California Press, 1993, p. 57.

2. Quoted in Reid, *Redefining Black Film*, p. 60.

filmmakers instead of major studios. In 1959's *Shadows*, for example, a light-skinned black woman and a white man fall in love. In a twist from the typical plots of similar films, the woman does not disclose her ethnicity—not because she is ashamed of being black, but because she assumes that it does not matter. Sadly, she finds out otherwise when her boyfriend deserts her after learning the truth.

In 1963, *The Cool World* looked at the subculture of youth gangs in New York City's Harlem district, portrayed as a culture of drugs and violence, largely ignored by the rich white people who live just a few blocks away. Another often-ignored subject—interracial marriage—was taken up in *One Potato, Two Potato* in 1964. In this film, a white woman divorces a white man, with whom she has a child, and marries a black man. America's fear of interracial couples is shown when custody of the wife's daughter is awarded to the girl's white biological father, despite the fact that he had deserted her and her mother. In 1964, a film titled *Nothing but a Man* spoke out against both white discrimination in the South and also the fear and timidity of black people who allowed racist practices to continue.

The general attitude of mainstream Hollywood toward blacks is best reflected in a series of highly successful Sidney Poitier films, starting with *Lilies of the Field* in 1963, which earned him the first Best Actor Academy Award ever for a black actor. His character is not a revolutionary role, however; he is again the lone black man in an all-white group. This time, he plays a traveling construction worker who encounters a band of nuns who believe he has been sent by God to help them build a chapel. His character was the perfect black hero for white audiences: warmhearted, earnest, dependable, nonthreatening, and, most importantly, ready to leave when the job is done.

Role Restrictions

Some black critics pointed out that Poitier's role in *Lilies of the Field* was not far from that of a servant. The same was true in his next two major films, *The Slender Thread* and *A Patch of Blue*, both released in 1965. In the former, he is a volunteer at a crisis clinic who answers a phone call from a woman who has taken pills to commit suicide. He keeps her on the phone until she can be rescued. Although race plays no part in the plot, Poitier's role is that of an assistant. In *A Patch of Blue*, he befriends a blind white teenage girl, once more playing a character who is there to be an assistant. In both of these films, his characters are not written to be forceful or equal to the white characters who share the screen.

In 1967, Poitier starred in *To Sir, with Love* as a teacher in an integrated English high school. This was

"I WAS A ONE-MAN SHOW"

In 1964, Sidney Poitier became the first African American to win the Academy Award for Best Actor, which he earned for his role in *Lilies of the Field*. While some saw his victory as a turning point in American race relations, Poitier disagreed:

> *Did I say to myself, "This country is waking up and beginning to recognize that certain changes are inevitable"? No, I did not. I knew that we hadn't "overcome," because I was still the only one. My career was unique in all of Hollywood. I knew that I was a one-man show, and it simply shouldn't be that way. And yet in a way I found the [award] itself quite natural. I wasn't surprised that such good things were happening to me, because I'd never seen myself as less than I am. When I realized that I could be a [great] actor, I realized that I had the responsibility, not as a black man, but as an artist, to exercise tremendous discipline. I knew the public would take my measure, and that was constantly in my calculations.*[1]

1. Sidney Poitier, *The Measure of a Man: A Spiritual Autobiography*. San Francisco, CA: HarperCollins, 2001, p. 107.

a far cry from his role as a juvenile delinquent in *The Blackboard Jungle*. While race is mentioned a few times, it is not a focus of the film, and Poitier, according to a *New York Times* review, "gives a quaint example of being proper and turning the other cheek ... there is little intrusion of or discussion about the issue of race."[53]

Perhaps the film that best embodied Poitier's style, as well as Hollywood's approach to race in the 1960s, is *Guess Who's Coming to Dinner*, which was released in 1967. This immensely popular movie begins with the engagement of a black man and white woman and focuses on their parents' reactions to the young couple's announcement. Despite the serious themes raised by the script, the film is played mostly as a comedy. One character sums things up by saying, "Civil rights is one thing but this here is something else," and the

New York Times review argued that the film "seems to be about something much more serious and challenging than it actually is."[54]

Pioneer or Villain?

As *Guess Who's Coming to Dinner* premiered in 1967, racial violence was erupting in major cities across America, and the question in many minds was whether blacks and whites could coexist peacefully. Many critics believed that the movie was out of step with the time period and so was Poitier. In a 1967 article, *New York Times* writer Clifford Mason published an article titled, "Why Does White America Love Sidney Poitier So?" Mason's conclusion was that he specialized in sympathetic, unthreatening roles, which were "essentially the same role, the [clean], one-dimensional hero."[55] Mason's criticism argued that even one of Poitier's most aggressive roles of the decade, as a black detective helping to solve a murder in 1967's *In the Heat of the Night*, was uninspired and unreal.

Some critics claimed that Poitier exemplified the past. The future for African Americans was represented by Jim Brown, a professional football legend who retired at the peak of his game and went into movies. As a large black man in an era when white people did not like aggres-

Jim Brown was an extremely talented running back in the National Football League until he retired. After his retirement, he played a number of characters in Hollywood films, typically in tough, aggressive roles.

sive black roles, Brown starred in such films as *The Dirty Dozen* in 1967, *Ice Station Zebra* in 1968, and *Riot* in 1969. Many of his roles were similar to those played by Poitier: He was commonly the lone black man in a white group. Brown, however, was always the man of action in the group; he was quick to use raw, physical power as well

A CRITICAL RESPONSE

In 1967, shortly after Sidney Poitier played an upper-middle class black intellectual in *Guess Who's Coming to Dinner*, Clifford Mason wrote an article for the *New York Times* titled "Why Does White America Love Sidney Poitier So?" Mason's point was that Poitier was not helping the cause of black Americans by playing such tame roles. In his autobiography, Poitier replied to this criticism:

All I can say is that there's a place for people who are angry and defiant, and sometimes they serve a purpose, but that's never been my role. And I have to say, too, that I have great respect for the kinds of people who are able to recycle their anger and put it to different uses. On the other hand, even Martin Luther King Jr. and Mahatma Gandhi, who certainly didn't appear angry when they burst upon the world, would have never burst upon the world in the first place if they hadn't, at one time in their lives, gone through much, much anger and much, much resentment, and much, much anguish.[1]

1. Sidney Poitier, *The Measure of a Man: A Spiritual Autobiography*. San Francisco, CA: HarperCollins, 2001, p. 124.

as his cunning mind. Black audiences responded to Brown's heroes the way white viewers did to Sean Connery's James Bond character—he was widely loved.

Violent Attitudes

Jim Brown was not alone in reflecting the growing aggression of the late 1960s. A series of films, starting with *Up Tight* in 1968, highlighted the increasing rejection of integration in black America. While *Up Tight* showed black guerrilla fighters in the streets of Cleveland, Ohio, *The Learning Tree*, released in 1969, took a less confrontational tone. In this film, Gordon Parks, the first black director of a major American film, tells the story of his boyhood in Kansas. The story is still brutal and challenging, as the creek where he swims turns red with the blood of a murdered black man.

The increasing willingness of Hollywood to take on sensitive racial themes was further exemplified by

The Great White Hope in 1970. This fictionalized story of black boxer Jack Johnson and his romantic relationships with white women won James Earl Jones an Academy Award nomination for Best Actor, the first for black actor since Poitier.

The last years of the decade were filled with social upheaval and protest—much of it angry, and some of it violent. "In 1960, Negroes were quietly asking for their [civil] rights," one historian wrote. "By 1969, blacks were demanding them."[56] The civil rights movement's highly visible spokesman for nonviolent protest, Martin Luther King Jr., was assassinated in 1968, and some African American leaders, such as Stokely Carmichael and H. Rap Brown, grabbed the spotlight to preach a different message: violent rejection of white-dominated society. It was time for a new type of black film, and this time, Hollywood was ready.

CHAPTER SIX

A NEW ERA OF FILMS

The 1960s were an uneven decade for African Americans. While some black movie stars, such as Sidney Poitier, rose to prominence by playing complicated and nuanced roles, Hollywood had still not let go of old stereotypes. Meanwhile, outside of the motion picture industry, the American civil rights movement was undergoing its own changes. Though Martin Luther King Jr. and other activists had encouraged nonviolent protests for racial equality, the assassination of King led some more violent groups to expand operations nationwide. By the end of the 1960s, America was a nation openly struggling with questions of race and equality.

Simultaneously, the movie industry was beginning to allow greater freedoms to black actors, directors, and producers. The growing anger of black people all over the country was reflected in the early 1970s, which saw a steady stream of films that glorified extreme violence and over-the-top action sequences by black main characters. Most critics believed that these movies had little artistic value and were merely an outpouring of years of anger against white society. This movement has since been named blaxploitation, which is a play on the fact that many people believed that the movies exploited black people to generate profits. They also created a new brand of stereotypes against African Americans.

Sweet Sweetback

Though the blaxploitation movement died down after a few years and Hollywood moved toward a more progressive stance on black people in film, it was powerful in the first few years of the 1970s. The director who made the first of these films in 1971, titled *Sweet Sweetback's Baadasssss*

Song, was Melvin Van Peebles. After working in the industry for a number of years, Van Peebles said he wanted "to do a movie that told it like it is. How I saw things."[57] The film featured a huge amount of violence and sexual material, all centered around the main character, played by Van Peebles, named Sweetback. Though it was little more sophisticated than an action thriller, it was a bold move for a black producer to take. One historian wrote that the film "changed the course of African American film production and the depiction of African Americans on screen."[58]

The film follows the life of Sweetback after he murders two white policemen who are beating a defenseless black youth. Rejecting a predictable ending in which Sweetback is killed or captured, Van Peebles allows his hero to escape after a series of scenes filled with violence. Sweetback is not sorry for what he has done, and there is no hidden moral to the story. The theme of the movie is not racial equality, but rather a tough black man "who challenges the oppressive white system and wins ... articulating the main feature of the Blaxploitation formula."[59]

The film opened in 1971 in only a few theaters but soon caught on with black audiences and was especially popular among young men. The word spread, and Van Peebles's film eventually generated more than $10 million. The movie appalled most reviewers, black and white alike. It was not artistic or polished, choosing to focus on intense violence and other graphic themes. Among black critics, it was especially repulsive. Not only was the main character an ultraviolent criminal, but the film encouraged the black community

Melvin Van Peebles was a groundbreaking African American filmmaker. Though Sweet Sweetback *was controversial when it released in 1971, it started a flood of similar movies over the next five years.*

MELVIN VAN PEEBLES

Melvin Van Peebles's *Sweet Sweetback's Baadasssss Song* was a surprise hit in 1971 and a huge financial success for Van Peebles, who had retained ownership of the film's negatives (which means he owned the original). In an interview many years later, he said his success was more due to poverty than to business sense:

People talk about Sweetback. *Man, I was just hoping I would get the money back so that the people I had borrowed from, buddies of mine, wouldn't kill me. No biggie. People say, "You're such a financial wizard. With* Sweetback *you own the film negative." I said, "I ain't got partners. Not because I was brilliant, but because nobody would do it with me." I played the role of Sweetback not for any reason except that I could find no one who would play it for me who knew anything about cinema. An actor would say, "Put in a few more lines for Sweetback." I'd say, "Well, he doesn't talk a lot." ... I invented the whole thing because I had no money.*[1]

1. Quoted in George Alexander, *Why We Make Movies: Black Filmmakers Talk About the Magic of Cinema.* New York, NY: Harlem Moon, 2003, pp. 21, 24.

to fear and hate whites. This only deepened racial divisions. One black observer, however, argued that such a shocking film was "[a necessary] step for anyone who wants to go further and make the first revolutionary black film."[60]

More Blaxploitation

Other films tried to quickly capitalize on *Sweet Sweetback*'s success. Gordon Parks moved from the slow dramatic pace of *The Learning Tree* in 1969 to the up-tempo *Shaft* in 1971, starring Richard Roundtree as a detective clad in black leather who does things his own way. John Shaft was a new kind of black hero who not only refused to be intimidated by whites, but also rejected the model of fitting into white society embodied in Sidney Poitier's roles.

Shaft was an even bigger box office success than *Sweet Sweetback*, thanks in part to its Academy Award-winning musical score by Isaac Hayes. The movie did well with both black and white audiences but was particularly popular with inner-city black viewers. To African American youth, who had lived in a system of oppression for their whole lives, detective Shaft looked "like a brother they had all seen many times before but never on the screen."[61]

The third groundbreaking film in

**Never a dude like this one!
He's got a plan to stick it to The Man!**

Super Fly, released in 1972, is one of the most famous films to come from the blaxploitation movement. Its main character was a drug dealer, and many have criticized the movie because it reinforced stereotypes of black people being criminals.

the blaxploitation genre was 1972's *Super Fly*, directed by Parks's son, Gordon Parks Jr. It went a step further than *Sweet Sweetback* and *Shaft* in that the hero, named Youngblood Priest, is an ordinary street criminal—a cocaine dealer in New York City. He is not a rebel, and he does not have a political agenda. He just wants to make as much money as he can and get out alive, which he manages to do.

The themes at work in *Super Fly* directly contradict integration films, which encouraged cooperation, compassion, and patience. Instead, *Super Fly* glorifies the idea that the end justifies the means, even if those means are illegal and involve getting ahead at others' expense. Moreover, *Super Fly* played into stereotypes that black people were commonly drug dealers who did not care about anything but money and violence.

Another common aspect of *Sweet Sweetback*, *Shaft*, and *Super Fly* is that women are frequently objectified. They are treated as possessions, not treated as people. Some films around the same time, however, featured black women in roles similar to Shaft and Priest. Pam Grier and Tamara Dobson play forceful and deadly parts in such films as *Foxy Brown* and *Cleopatra Jones*, but unlike most of their male counterparts, they have respectable

SOUND ADVICE

Gordon Parks had already established his credentials as an award-winning photographer for *LIFE* magazine when he turned to filmmaking in 1964. His autobiographical 1969 film *The Learning Tree* won critical praise, but his biggest hit was *Shaft* in 1971. When asked what advice he would give young directors, he replied:

To do anything well, you have to have a purpose other than just money. You have to have good feelings about the universe, about people, about helping it become a better universe ... I try to make my day worthwhile, my life worthwhile. If you don't have good thoughts about good things, you'll never make good photographs. You're not going to make good pictures and you're not going to write good books or anything else. You're not going to write good music. You might think that you're being successful but in the end you're not unless you're making some sincere contribution—especially to our youth, because our youth are tomorrow. Without our youth, there is no tomorrow.[1]

1. Quoted in George Alexander, *Why We Make Movies: Black Filmmakers Talk About the Magic of Cinema*. New York, NY: Harlem Moon, 2003, p. 14.

goals, such as clearing up the drug trade in their neighborhoods.

Exploiting Blaxploitation

The success of the early blaxploitation films led to a steady stream of imitators. Between 1971 and 1974, hundreds of American movies followed the blaxploitation formula. That does not mean they originated in the black community, however. A huge portion of them were written, directed, and produced by whites.

Many African American leaders were outraged by the constant stream of thugs, drug dealers, and criminals across the nation's screens and accused white filmmakers of sensationalism and exploitation. Their protests had little effect, but blaxploitation eventually turned into its own worst enemy. Plots kept repeating themselves, characters were unoriginal, audiences grew bored, profits shrank, and filmmakers turned to other projects. Blaxploitation films, though, had made their mark, leaving a specific image of stereotypical urban black culture in the public mind.

It was not, however, the only image. Although there were few good roles for black women, two actresses were able to rise above the crowd. Diana Ross, former lead singer in the Motown group the Supremes, scored a Best Actress Academy Award nomination in 1973 for 1972's *Lady Sings the Blues*, a fictionalized biography of jazz singer Billie Holiday. In 1974, Diahann Carroll received a Best Actress Academy Award nomination for *Claudine*, which told the story of the struggles of an African American mother on welfare in New York City.

Diana Ross rose to fame as an extraordinarily talented singer, actress, and all-around entertainer. She was nominated for an Academy Award in the category of Best Actress for her portrayal of Billie Holiday in Lady Sings the Blues.

Powerful and Funny

One of Ross's rivals for the 1973 Academy Award was another black actress, Cicely Tyson, for *Sounder*. That film, set in the South during the Great Depression of the 1930s, movingly portrayed the strong bonds of love and respect among members of a black farm family. This was one of the first such depictions of African American family life. It earned Academy Award nominations for not only Tyson, but also for black screenwriter Lonnie Elder III and for Paul Winfield, who played the family father, for Best Actor. It was also nominated for Best Picture.

The primary focus of black films in the later years of blaxploitation, however, was comedy. The groundwork had been laid in 1972 with the success of *Buck and the Preacher*, which marked the debut of Sidney Poitier as a director. He also co-starred in the film with Harry Belafonte. They played two freed slaves who outwit the whites who attempt to return them to slavery. Though there is obvious racial tension in the film, it is nearly canceled out by the comic relief that runs throughout.

Buck and the Preacher did not get good reviews, and Poitier was wise enough in subsequent 1970s comedies, such as *Uptown Saturday Night*, *Let's Do It Again*, and *Stir Crazy*, to leave most of the comic relief to more experienced comedians. He acted in the first two, but those films were supported by famous black comics, such as Flip Wilson and the emerging black star of the decade, Richard Pryor.

The End of Blaxploitation

Pryor was hardly a newcomer by the time he acted in *Stir Crazy*. He had been performing as a nightclub comedian since 1963 and had perfected an image of someone who would say and do anything, no matter how outrageous or offensive it was. It was the kind of character that he could not have played on screen, but he still came across as wild and utterly unpredictable. He was just as hostile toward authority as Sweetback, but instead of playing a hardened criminal who killed easily, he was crazy and did anything he wanted.

His first part in a major film was the serious dramatic role of the edgy drug addict Piano Man in *Lady Sings the Blues*, which won him some degree of critical respect. Cowriting and acting credits in a number of comedy films followed, including *Car Wash*, before Pryor teamed up with Gene Wilder in *Silver Streak* in 1976. His depiction of Grover Muldoon, a quick-witted, fast-talking thief, made Pryor a major star.

Not even Pryor's talents, however,

As a Broadway musical, The Wiz *is wildly popular to this day. When the 1978 film adaptation was released, however, its performance was disastrous. It was poorly received by both critics and audiences.*

could save *The Wiz*, the 1978 film adaptation of the all-black Broadway hit. At a cost of $24 million, it was the most expensive musical made to date. With an all-star cast that included Pryor, Diana Ross, Lena Horne, Nipsey Russell, and Michael Jackson, it seemed poised to be an immense success.

Even with a huge budget and talented actors, it was a failure. Reviewers aggressively criticized *The Wiz*, many complaining that Ross, at 34, was just too old for the role of a young Dorothy. Film historian Charles Harpole called it "one of the decade's biggest failures."[62] It was a commercial disaster as well, making back barely half of its production costs in its theatrical run.

The combination of bad reviews and financial losses may have convinced Hollywood that there was no longer a profitable audience for blaxploitation movies. Such films, which had been a fixture of the mid-1970s, all but vanished in the next decade. Roles for black actors declined overall and were mostly limited to supporting parts during the next few years. Academy Award nominations mirrored this trend, though some black actors in the 1980s received nominations or won the coveted award.

An Emerging Genre

Many of the supporting roles came in what are called buddy movies. These showed the unlikely pairing of two people, often from significantly different walks of life, who reach mutual understanding and respect. Black-white pairings in this genre had been very successful—from 1957's *Edge of the City* to 1958's *The Defiant Ones* to 1976's *Silver Streak*.

The wide variety in these supporting roles is evident in *An Officer and a Gentleman* in 1982, *Lethal Weapon* in 1987, and *Driving Miss Daisy* in 1989. In the first, Louis Gossett Jr. plays a strict black drill sergeant who goads and motivates an arrogant white recruit into becoming a competent and successful naval aviator. The film is unusual in that the black man is in the position of authority, yelling at the white man and calling him "boy." The role won Gossett the Academy Award for Best Supporting Actor.

Similar is the relationship between Danny Glover's black policeman and his white counterpart Mel Gibson in *Lethal Weapon*, a pairing so successful it spawned several sequels over the years. Unlike many police stories that paired a reckless black officer with a calm white one, in the *Lethal Weapon* series, Glover is the steadying influence on his wild partner, the white Gibson. Glover received an NAACP Image Award for his performance.

In *Driving Miss Daisy*, Morgan

Freeman took on the type of role that goes all the way back to Mammy in *Gone with the Wind*—that of the black servant of a rich and proper southern lady, who treats him as a confidant and friend but only within strict boundaries. In this case, Freeman is Hoke Colburn, chauffeur for several decades to an elderly white widow played by Jessica Tandy. Freeman and Tandy's interactions provide some gentle commentary on racism, as Hoke

maintains the proper relationship with his employer but still maintains his dignity and independence. *Driving Miss Daisy* was one of the most popular films of the 1980s, with both critical and commercial success. Freeman received an Academy Award nomination for Best Actor, Tandy won the Academy Award for Best Actress, and the movie won the award for Best Picture.

African American Comedians

Another black actor who rose to stardom in buddy roles was comedian and actor Eddie Murphy. In 1982's *48 Hours*, he plays a convict released from prison to help a racist white policeman, played by Nick Nolte, solve a case. He refuses to be intimidated by Nolte's racist remarks and instead fires insults right back at his white partner, who eventually comes to respect him. A year later, Murphy teamed with white actor and fellow *Saturday Night Live* veteran Dan Aykroyd in *Trading Places*, a comedy in which a poor African American conman and a wealthy white snob suddenly find themselves in each other's circumstances.

Already famous for his acting abilities, Morgan Freeman continued his career of excellence as Hoke in Driving Miss Daisy *in 1989. The movie was one of the most successful of the decade.*

Murphy went on to become one of the most popular entertainment acts, of any race, of the 1980s. His most successful film of that decade was *Beverly*

Hills Cop, the story of a Detroit policeman who fast-talks his way through an investigation in the wealthy California neighborhood of Beverly Hills. Far from being impressed by the people he encounters, he uses his race as a weapon, throwing it in their faces and watching them get intimidated by him. His character, Axel Foley, proved so popular that three sequels of *Beverly Hills Cop* were made, some more than 20 years after the original.

Although Murphy and many other black men achieved success in the 1980s, it was not as prosperous a time for black women in film. Few movie studios offered black actresses roles in which they could make an impact. The major exception was *The Color Purple* in 1985, which emerged as the most controversial African American film of the decade.

Color Controversy

Based on Alice Walker's Pulitzer Prize–winning novel, *The Color Purple* explores abusive relationships between black women and black men. Whoopi Goldberg, playing the long-suffering Celie, was the only black actress nominated for an Academy Award in a leading role in the 1980s. Her costars, Margaret Avery and Oprah Winfrey, were also nominated for their supporting roles in the film.

Controversy arose over the film's depiction of black men, which some critics labeled one-sided. Their portrayal as aggressive and stupid, some argued, was just as wrong in 1985 as it was 70 years earlier in *The Birth of a Nation*. At the same time, the film boldly examined domestic abuse, which was an unpleasant topic to put on screen. Critics and audiences were split over

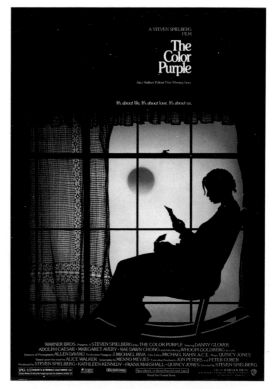

The Color Purple remains one of the most influential movies about African Americans ever produced. It was a blockbuster film when it was released in 1985, and it helped revive the role of black people in Hollywood.

The Color Purple. This indecision was evident when the film failed to win any Oscars despite its 11 nominations.

Although *The Color Purple* was one of the only blockbuster black-themed movies of the 1980s, several others were based on race relations. Although black actors enjoyed a few prominent roles, many of these stories concentrated more on the white experience. For instance, *Cry Freedom*, a 1987 feature about South African activist Steve Biko, earned Denzel Washington an Oscar nomination for Best Supporting Actor. However, much of the movie was centered around his character's white journalist friend. Likewise, when Washington won the Best Supporting Actor Academy Award for *Glory* in 1989, most of the plot of that film was focused not on the African American Civil War soldiers, but on their white officer.

Just before the end of the decade, however, a new major motion picture star arrived on the scene. He did not make his name as an actor, however—he was widely renowned as a director and producer. In 1986, not long after earning a master's degree in film and television studies from New York University, a unique new African American director made his presence known with the surprise hit *She's Gotta Have It*. His name was Shelton Jackson Lee, better known as Spike. His films shook up the industry, took it in a bold direction in the coming decades, and revolutionized the way America thought of black people in film.

CHAPTER SEVEN
SPIKE LEE AND A NEW WAVE OF MOTION PICTURES

For most of the 1970s and 1980s, African Americans in the film industry had taken relatively few steps forward. Although large organizations, such as the Academy of Motion Picture Arts and Sciences, which awards the Oscars, had been more inclusive of black professionals as the years went on, most black roles were still uninspired or subtly prejudicial. Hollywood had still not decided whether African Americans would be an integral part of the movie industry. This began to change with a wave of new black stars.

Some of the most prominent actors from the late 20th century were, in fact, African American. From Eddie Murphy's comedic roles to the serious and dramatic talents of Denzel Washington, millions of Americans were beginning to appreciate black actors for their work—their acting—rather than their skin color. By the time the 1990s came around, a man named Spike Lee was breaking the gates of the movie industry wide open and encouraging other black professionals to join in.

Many of the films made by or starring African Americans during this decade were challenging and complicated. They addressed dark themes and explored previously forbidden areas of American culture. However, the new waves of filmmakers and actors were also capable of being funny and self-aware. The most prominent of these figures was Spike Lee, whose films, beginning in 1986 with *She's Gotta Have It*, were telling bold and original stories in a unique and groundbreaking way. His work dragged race and other social issues directly into the spotlight for everyone to see. Though this was controversial on its own, critics and audiences had an extremely strong reaction to his 1989 film titled *Do the Right Thing*.

A VIOLENT TIME

Spike Lee's first two major films, *She's Gotta Have It* and *School Daze*, did not prepare viewers for the violent conclusion to *Do the Right Thing*, which ends with a racially motivated riot. He decided to make the film take a darker turn after hearing a news report about an assault on two black youths in a white neighborhood in New York City. He stated,

While I was in the [store] today, I heard a radio newscast that two Black youths had been beaten up by a gang of white youths in Bensonhurst. The two Black kids were hospitalized. They were collecting bottles and cans when they got jumped. This happened on Christmas night. Just the other day some Black kids fired up a white cab driver in Harlem. New York City is tense with racial hatred. Can you imagine if these incidents had taken place in the summer, on the hottest day of the year? I'd be a fool not to work the subject of racism into 'Do the Right Thing.'[1]

1. Quoted in Mark A. Reid, *Redefining Black Film*. Los Angeles, CA: University of California Press, 1993, p. 104.

This movie is a critical examination of racial tensions in New York City. Lee sets the scene to be as believable as possible, including dozens of extras to make the city lifelike, and he slowly builds racial tension between whites and blacks throughout the film. Things come to a head with the accidental death of a young African American at the hands of a white police officer. A large portion of the end of the movie shows a riot that is instigated by Lee's character out of anger.

Acclaim and Fear

Chicago Sun-Times reviewer Roger Ebert wrote that *Do the Right Thing* "comes closer to reflecting the current state of race relations in America than any other movie of our time."[63] Other reviewers did not approve of the portrayal of violence, and some civic leaders worried that it would spark riots in real life. At the heart of the controversy was a question: Was Lee condemning the violence or excusing it as justified? The ending of the film, just before the credits roll, shows opposing quotations on violence from Martin Luther King Jr. and Malcolm X. King's quotation discourages violence, while Malcolm X's quotation gives it an excuse. By concluding his movie like this, Lee seemed to want people to make their own decisions about it.

Lee would go on to make dozens of feature films on every aspect of African American culture, with topics ranging from sports (*He Got Game*, 1998) to music (*Mo' Better Blues*, 1990) to political activism (*Get on the Bus*, 1996). Many of them were controversial, but none more than 1992's *Malcolm X*, which was based on the autobiography of the inflammatory African American leader who was assassinated in 1965. Some people said the movie glorified Malcolm X too much; others said it did not glorify him enough. As usual, Lee seemed to be an observer, presenting the story and letting viewers draw their own conclusions.

Publicly, however, Lee was always quick to speak out against Hollywood's hesitancy to make serious black films and, when it did, black audiences' refusal to support them. He frequently commented on the genre of black films that Hollywood would produce. In the 1990s, he claimed that studios refused to make any films about black historical figures or cast black actors

Spike Lee is a groundbreaking filmmaker, and his movies about race relations have been widely praised by people of all races. He has received an Honorary Academy Award and earned accolades from many other organizations.

outside of roles of drug dealers or criminals. Such comments have alienated Hollywood insiders from Lee and may be a factor in keeping him from the Academy Awards. He has only been nominated twice: for Best Screenplay for *Do the Right Thing* in 1990 and for Best Documentary for *4 Little Girls* in 1998, but in 2015, he was given an Honorary Academy Award.

EXPOSING RACISM

In the months following the release of Spike Lee's *Do the Right Thing*, some critics complained that the portrayal of white racists and the violence at the film's conclusion were upsetting to many white viewers. To this, Lee replied,

How do you think Black people have felt for 80 years watching stuff like Birth of a Nation . . . and we go on and on. Black people have had to live under this thing for 400 years. If white people have to [feel uncomfortable] for two hours watching this film, that's great. I think it's a good kind of [uncomfortable], because for the most part the movies today are just mindless entertainment; they don't make you think. We made this film so we could put the spotlight on racism and say everything is NOT okay, that this is not the land of milk and honey and truth and justice. We should stop hiding from the issue of racism.[1]

1. Quoted in Jesse Algeron Rhines, *Black Film/White Money*. New Brunswick, NJ: Rutgers University Press, 1996, p. 112.

Inspiring Others

Several black directors were quick to follow Lee's lead. Immediately after he saw *Do the Right Thing*, John Singleton went to work on the screenplay for *Boyz n the Hood*, a 1991 story about gang violence in Los Angeles. The film earned Singleton Academy Award nominations for Best Director—and for Best Screenplay.

The same year saw the release of *New Jack City*, produced and directed by Melvin Van Peebles' son, Mario. There are similarities between Mario's film and his father's *Sweet Sweetback*.

Both are uncompromising views of inner-city life. The key difference is that, while the Sweetback character fights against the law and succeeds, *New Jack City*'s main character, Nino, is gunned down at the film's end. This theme—urban crime and violence as a dead end—would show up in many movies during the 1990s.

A similar fate awaits black gang leader Slim in 1991's *A Rage in Harlem*, directed by Bill Duke. Also, Caine, the young drug dealer character in 1993's *Menace II Society*, directed by Albert and Allen Hughes, tries to escape the

HELPING EQUALITY

Bill Duke followed a successful career as an actor in *Car Wash*, *Menace II Society*, *Predator*, and other films, with an equally successful career as a director. In addition to *A Rage in Harlem*, he has directed television episodes of *Hill Street Blues*, *Miami Vice*, and *Fame*.

In 1998, Duke began a program of mentoring young African Americans pursuing careers in motion pictures. Classes of 35 aspiring actors or directors attended a 10-week seminar "to study acting and industry survival techniques."[1] His skill as a teacher earned him an appointment as chair of the Department of Radio, Television, and Film at Howard University in Washington, D.C.

Duke has visionary ideas about how to expand racial commentary in films. Rather than focusing specifically on a racial component, he has talked about how he would approach these new portrayals:

> There are a lot of films I want to make about America, films that have to do with issues that affect black people, but don't involve them. They happen in corporate offices and in halls of justice, in congressional halls—the politics of this country. Black people have no access to this reality. Those are things I want to talk about, the films I want to make ... I want to be able to make a film ... because I'm the best director for the film.[2]

1. Quoted in Melvin Donalson, *Black Directors in Hollywood*. Austin, TX: University of Texas Press, 2003, p. 287.

2. Quoted in Melvin Donalson, *Black Directors in Hollywood*, p. 287.

ghetto and make a new life but is killed in a drive-by shooting. Such films portray the harsh reality of violence that this new wave of black directors wanted to bring to public attention. Harvard University professor Henry Louis Gates commented on the extreme violence depicted on the screen, and defended it: "You don't know whether you're watching a nightmare or the nightly news."[64] Films such as these were the only way millions of white Americans saw the underbelly of urban black life.

New Perspectives

Not all the new black films in the

1990s concentrated on modern ghetto life, however. Carl Franklin's *Devil in a Blue Dress* in 1995 is set in South Central Los Angeles in the 1940s. It is an unusual crime-thriller that is reminiscent of the private detective films of that era—except that it is from a black point of view. George Tillman Jr.'s 1997 *Soul Food* is a gentle story about love and tensions between members of a middle-class African American family in Chicago. The film proved that there were compelling black stories to be told beyond the inner city. Melvin Donalson, a film historian, called it "one of the most memorable films to present contemporary black family life."[65]

Moreover, the aggressive attitudes of black films seemed to have significantly mellowed during the 1990s. Perhaps the best example was *The Best Man* in 1999, which was directed by Spike Lee's younger cousin, Malcolm Lee. The film avoided the inner city setting of older black films, focusing on educated, middle-class black professionals, including a novelist, a social worker, and a television producer. It is a movie about African Americans, but is not a "black" movie. The characters have human problems, not problems that are specific to African Americans. The film is so different from those of Spike Lee, who coproduced it, that *Village Voice* critic Amy Taubin wrote that Spike "has never directed a film that goes down as easily as this one does."[66]

A New Generation of Black Actors

The new wave of black films in the 1990s provided new opportunities for a number of African American actors. Denzel Washington was already famous for his work in 1987's *Cry Freedom* and *Glory*, but he earned two more Academy Award nominations between 1990 and 2000—for *Malcolm X* in 1993 and *The Hurricane* in 2000—and lead roles in such hits as *Mo' Better Blues*, *The Pelican Brief*, *Crimson Tide*, and *He Got Game*. Handsome and well-spoken, he was a favorite of female audiences. However, like other black actors before him, he was given few romantic roles in a film industry that was still reluctant to show African American male sexuality.

Morgan Freeman solidified his status as one of America's most popular actors, earning an Academy Award nomination for Best Actor as a veteran convict in *The Shawshank Redemption* in 1994. Also earning a Best Actor nomination was Laurence Fishburne for his role as singer Ike Turner in 1993's *What's Love Got to Do with It*. Fishburne was in great demand for his talents, appearing in nearly 20 films in

Denzel Washington is one of the most recognizable faces in Hollywood. He has played a variety of roles—from African American activist Malcolm X in 1992 (shown here) to Coach Boone in Remember the Titans *in 2000.*

the 1990s. His roles were diverse, as he played characters from urban father Furious Styles in *Boyz n the Hood* to 16th-century soldier Othello in the film adaptation of the Shakespeare play of the same name.

Less-established actors who made names for themselves in the 1990s included Samuel L. Jackson, Cuba Gooding Jr., Wesley Snipes, and Will Smith. Jackson had been a staple in

Spike Lee's films, but his career really took off after he played Jules Winnfield, the religious hit man in *Pulp Fiction* in 1994. The performance earned him an Academy Award nomination for Best Supporting Actor, and he has gone on to play prominent roles in dozens of movies. Cuba Gooding Jr. won the Academy Award for Best Supporting Actor for his role as a professional football player in 1996's *Jerry Maguire*.

Like Jackson, Wesley Snipes appeared in several early Spike Lee films, but he began to draw critical acclaim when he played Nino, the drug kingpin in *New Jack City*, a role that was especially written for him. He played many diverse characters during the 1990s, including a basketball hustler in *White Men Can't Jump*, a paraplegic in *The Waterdance*, and a detective sidekick to Sean Connery in *Rising Sun*. He achieved his greatest success as both an action hero, playing a policeman in *Boiling Point* and a vampire hunter in the *Blade* series, and an action villain, playing crime boss Simon Phoenix in *Demolition Man*.

Will Smith was best known for his lead role in television's popular *The Fresh Prince of Bel-Air* before making a name for himself in back-to-back big-screen hits as the confident fight pilot in *Independence Day* in 1996 the alien-hunting government age

Will Smith made the leap from the small screen onto the big screen in the 1990s. Since then, he has become one of the most successful African American actors of all time.

the romantic fantasy-thriller *Ghost* in 1990. She plays a fake spiritualist named Oda who is terrified when she is actually contacted by the ghost of Sam, played by Patrick Swayze. She overcomes her fear, becomes a link between Sam and his still-living girlfriend, and helps prevent a crime. Janet Maslin wrote in the *New York Times*, "Ms. Goldberg has found a film role that really suits her, and she makes the most of it."[67] Others agreed, and Goldberg became just the second black woman ever to win an Academy Award for Best Supporting Actress.

Men in Black in 1997. He also proved that he was capable of playing a more serious lead role in 1998's *Enemy of the State* and ended the decade as one of Hollywood's biggest stars.

Underappreciated Actresses

Though African American men were highly-praised in 1990s, the decade was not as kind to black actresses. The years after *The Color Purple* had not been particularly rewarding for Goopi Goldberg, but that ended with

Other films focused more closely on the lives of black women. In 1991's *Daughters of the Dust*, black director Julie Dash portrays the conflicts among the women of a South Carolina family in 1902 as some members are preparing to move north. Much more modern—and commercially successful—was *Waiting to Exhale*, released in 1995. It tells the story of four black women and their relationships with one another and the men in their lives.

Directed by veteran black actor Forest Whitaker, the film found a large audience among black women and was a triumph for actress Angela Bassett.

Bassett was one of the most popular black actresses of the decade. She first came to the public's attention in *Boyz n the Hood* and then succeeded in a much more challenging role: Betty Shabazz in the 1992 film *Malcolm X*. She then played the role of pop singer Tina Turner in *What's Love Got to Do with It*, beating out other stars Halle Berry and Robin Givens for the part. Her performance, which one reviewer wrote, "shows off Bassett's ferocity and range,"[68] got her an Academy Award nomination. Bassett also received critical and popular acclaim as an older woman in love with a younger man in *How Stella Got Her Groove Back* in 1998.

Black women played lead roles in two other major feature films of the 1990s: *Eve's Bayou* in 1997 and *Beloved* in 1998. The first, directed by black actress Kasi Lemmons, tells the story of Eve, a young woman who tries to hold her family together through a series of revelations and troubles that end in tragedy. The film was hailed by critics as one of the finest of the decade, but received no Academy Award nominations; though critic Roger Ebert wrote, "If it is not nominated for Academy Awards, then the academy is not paying attention."[69]

Angela Bassett was a major movie star beginning in the 1990s. Critics and fans of all races praised her performances in difficult and varied roles.

Beloved by More

In 1998, *Beloved*, based on the Pulitzer Prize–winning novel of the same name by Toni Morrison, received much more attention than *Eve's Bayou*. This was mainly through the efforts of influential talk-show host and actress Oprah Winfrey, who produced and starred in the film. Winfrey plays Sethe, a former slave with a history of being

A POWERFUL VOICE

Few black artists in Hollywood have had as much success as Forest Whitaker. As an actor, he earned a Golden Globe nomination for Best Actor as saxophonist Charlie Bird in *Bird* and won the 2007 Academy Award for Best Actor as Idi Amin in *The Last King of Scotland*. He also directed the highly regarded *Waiting to Exhale* in 1995. In an interview, Whitaker gave his opinion on the power of motion pictures and the attention to detail that goes into making a film:

> *Movies can be [many] things because movies can transform ... By that I mean, in our country we can make people see something and understand something that they never did before ... So that's why you have to be careful as to what it is the director does and what it is the director says ... I think that I am disappointed in any filmmaker who [encourages] negative stereotypes be they Black, white, Mexican or whatever. Certainly, you would think that if it's of your own culture that you would have the sensitivity to know that what you might be doing could be [harmful] ... So for me, I would hope that Black filmmakers would have the sensitivity to what it is they're projecting [in a film] and how it can affect people.*[1]

1. Quoted in George Alexander, *Why We Make Movies: Black Filmmakers Talk About the Magic of Cinema.* New York, NY: Harlem Moon, 2003, pp. 487–488.

abused. Over the course of the film, it is revealed that when her former master tried to reclaim her, Sethe killed her daughter and tried to kill her other children rather than lose them to slavery. The drama revolves around the appearance, 10 years later, of a young woman who calls herself Beloved. Sethe believes that Beloved is symbolic of her deceased daughter.

Critics were divided in their opinions of *Beloved*, and audiences were largely disappointed. It did not make much money at the box office, and its lack of profits made Hollywood think twice before spending a lot of money on another serious film about African Americans. *Beloved* was not the only film that contributed to this development, however. In 1997, for example, a film titled *Amistad* was produced with a budget of more than $36 million. Though it told an interesting story about an 1839 mutiny aboard a slave ship, it was a financial failure.

The decade did contribute to the rise of several black actors who would reach stardom in the years to come. Halle Berry made her film debut in Spike Lee's *Jungle Fever* in 1991 and was featured in *Losing Isaiah* in 1995 and *Why Do Fools Fall in Love* in 1998. Jamie Foxx, who started his career in television sketch comedy, made a dramatic impression in 1999's big-screen hit *Any Given Sunday*. Queen Latifah made the leap from hip-hop to feature films with major roles in *Set It Off* in 1996 and *The Bone Collector* in 1999.

As the 20th century came to a close, African Americans in the motion picture industry were in the best position they had ever been. Major stars, from the dramatic Denzel Washington to the comedic Will Smith to the powerful Oprah Winfrey, rose to prominent positions in film and television during the 1990s. Moreover, influential directors and producers, such as Spike Lee, had laid a path for black people to take themselves even further in movies. Heading in the 21st century, the potential for African Americans was huge.

CHAPTER EIGHT

THE 2000s AND BEYOND

The new century brought with it high expectations for African Americans, both socially and in the film industry. A relatively large number of black movie stars, both actors and directors, had emerged during the 1990s, and the new millennium was ready to embrace their new work. At the same time, another new generation of movie professionals was stepping onto the scene, and new genres of movies were making black leading actors more profitable than ever.

Simultaneously, rap music was spreading across the country, as younger white Americans no longer attached a racist stigma to black musicians and songs about black culture. As a result, the early 2000s had an infusion of films about the lives of rap and hip-hop artists, most of which were popular and profitable. As successful as this new genre of rap films was, some critics and observers did not like the lifestyles that they encouraged. These complaints were echoes of those 30 years earlier about films such as *Super Fly*, which glorified a life of black crime and drug use.

Nevertheless, it was still a good time to be a black actor in Hollywood. As one historian wrote, "black actors … have risen in visibility and [profitability] in more mainstream leading-man roles."[70] Because young people in America were eager to see films with strong black main characters, those are the kinds of films the early 2000s produced.

Creating Opportunity

In 2002, for his performance as a crooked policeman in 2001's *Training Day*, Denzel Washington became the first African American honored with the Academy Award for Best Actor since Sidney Poitier nearly 40 years earlier. One of Washington's fellow nominees was Will Smith, who played the title role in Spike Lee's *Ali* in 2001, which told the story of black boxing legend Muhammad Ali.

Biographical films, in fact, were some of the most popular vehicles for black male stars in the 2000s. Jamie Foxx won an Academy Award for Best Actor for his portrayal of soul singer Ray Charles in *Ray* in 2005. One of his fellow nominees was Don Cheadle, honored for his performance in *Hotel Rwanda*, which is a gripping and tragic true story of the Rwandan genocide. Forest Whitaker won the Academy Award for Best Actor for his work in 2006's *The Last King of Scotland*, which is the story of dictator Idi Amin's rise to power in Uganda. Also nominated in the Best Actor category that year was Will Smith, for his performance in *The Pursuit of Happyness*.

At the 2005 Academy Awards ceremony, Foxx not only won for his role in *Ray*, but was also a nominee for Best Supporting Actor for his work in the film *Collateral*. The winner in that category was another huge African American star, Morgan Freeman, for his role as a boxing trainer in *Million Dollar Baby*.

Academy Award nominations also went to lesser-known black actors in the early years of the new century. Djimon Hounsou, a native of the West African country of Benin, was twice nominated for Best Supporting Actor, for *In America* in 2004 and *Blood Diamond* in 2007. Terrence Howard was a Best Actor nominee for his role as a Memphis pimp and aspiring hip-hop DJ in *Hustle & Flow* in 2006. Eddie Murphy, better known for his famous light comedies, earned a Best Supporting Actor nomination for his performance as R&B singer James "Thunder" Early in the 2006 musical *Dreamgirls*.

Between 2000 and 2017, black actors have been nominated nearly 20 times for Academy Awards in the categories of Best Actor and Best Supporting Actor. Black actresses have also done fairly well, being nominated for more than 15 awards in the same timespan. Also, in 2002, Halle Berry became the first black woman to win the Academy Award for Best Actress for her performance as the widow of an executed murderer in *Monster's Ball*.

Inequality and Action

Despite their critical acclaim, there were not many strong roles available to women in the early 2000s. "The rise of hip-hop and inner-city movies by and about black men has been almost exclusively a plus for men, not women," one historian reported in 2005. "They are not represented, either as producers or stars, the way men are."[71]

However, as the decade went on, black actresses began receiving more roles worthy of Academy Award nominations and victories. Musicals became a gateway to award-season success. Queen Latifah was nominated for her role in *Chicago,* and Jennifer Hudson was the winner of an Academy Award for *Dreamgirls.*

On the other end of the cinematic spectrum, *Hotel Rwanda*, *The Last King of Scotland*, and *Blood Diamond* were part of a trend in black films of this period: an interest in African history, politics, and culture. Others included *Lumumba*, about the Congolese leader assassinated in 1961, as well as the South African-themed *Tsotsi* in 2005 and *Catch a Fire* in 2006. "Africa has been underrepresented in our literature and our storytelling generally,"[72] said Kevin Macdonald, director of *The Last King of Scotland*. He noted that filmmakers are looking for fresh themes and locations, and Africa is a place filled with both.

At least one standard genre—action films—remained as popular as ever, even though many of the subjects had been seen before. Samuel L. Jackson starred in a 2000 remake of *Shaft*, Laurence Fishburne made three films in the *Matrix* series, and Wesley Snipes made two more films in the *Blade* series. *Training Day*, *Collateral*, and *I, Robot* were action-packed movies with African American leads, and Denzel Washington played a Harlem drug dealer in 2007's *American Gangster*. There were more thoughtful and engaging films, as well. Cuba Gooding Jr. was

Queen Latifah is just one of the African American actresses who has risen to prominence since the turn of the 21st century. She was nominated for an Academy Award for her performance in Chicago *in 2003.*

featured in two well-received movies about African Americans in the military: *Men of Honor* is the story of Carl Brashear, the first African American to become a U.S. Navy Master Diver; and *Pearl Harbor* featured the story of Dorie Miller, who was awarded the Navy Cross for his heroism during the Pearl Harbor attack.

Every Genre Represented

The comedians had their time to shine, too. Eddie Murphy made *Bowfinger*, *Norbit*, a remake of the 1960s comedy *The Nutty Professor*, and a sequel to that, *The Klumps*. Other hits for African American comics included *Head of State*, *Daddy Daycare*, and *Big Momma's House*, but the comedy considered most in tune with black culture was Spike Lee's *The Original Kings of Comedy*. This documentary took onstage and backstage looks at a tour in 2000 by comedians Steve Harvey, D.L. Hughley, Cedric the Entertainer, and Bernie Mac. Their routines about black culture and race relations were reminiscent of Richard Pryor's, and reviewer Esther Iverem praised the "old-school, pre-hip-hop sensibility in the culture."[73]

Other black films in the new century were not as easy to categorize. *Love and Basketball*, for example, is both a romantic story and a sports movie. *The Caveman's Valentine*, directed by Kasi Lemmons and starring Samuel L. Jackson, is the offbeat story of a mentally disturbed musician living in a New York City park. The critically acclaimed *Antwone Fisher* is about a young black man with a tormented childhood and his struggle to overcome the consequences of his past. He is helped by a psychiatrist played by

Kasi Lemmons is a successful actress and director. She has earned widespread praise for her work, including an NAACP Image Award, shown here.

Denzel Washington, who also directed the project.

What Is Progress?

As the 21st century continues and more black actors, filmmakers, and critics gain a foothold in Hollywood, the question remains: How much progress has been made since the days when the old racist stereotypes ruled the screen? There is no definite answer, partly because there is disagreement on what exactly that means. Is progress measured by the extent to which films accurately represent black culture, or is it measured by the extent to which films are colorblind? Should the goal be making movies specifically about African Americans or making movies about people who could be of any race?

Two films of the 2000s illustrate the debate. Spike Lee's *Bamboozled* is about a black television producer who is pressured into creating a blackface minstrel show. Black activists protest the show, and a radical group eventually kidnaps and kills one of its stars. The message is seemingly that black culture must prevail over stereotypes created to entertain whites.

The Pursuit of Happyness, in contrast, is the story of a homeless single father's relationship with his son as he tries to improve both of their lives. This true story about a black man, and starring a black actor, could easily be about a white man, starring a white actor. It treats the African American protagonists exactly the same as it would if the main characters were white or any other race.

One of the more controversial figures in modern African American motion pictures is Tyler Perry. He has been an actor, writer, director, and producer in a number of mainstream films that have been massively successful—at least financially. Critics of Perry have argued that his films are terrible stereotypes of black life, rather than real representations of African American racial struggles. Nonetheless, he has achieved massive commercial success as a major Hollywood producer.

Marked Improvements

Regardless of the interpretation of progress for African Americans in film, there is no doubt that the lives of black actors, producers, directors, and other motion picture professionals has drastically improved since the early 1900s. The portrayal of black people in movies has evolved noticeably in the more than 100 years since motion pictures first spread across the United States. From servant and slave characters, to clumsy fools, to criminals, and finally just to everyday people, nearly every decade has witnessed a transformation of African Americans on the big screen. Numerous films regarding race relations, some of them major Hollywood blockbuster features, are released every year, and countless modern films take up themes that would have been forbidden 40 years ago.

Black actors and actresses receive more equal recognition for their acting talents than they did in the early years of the film industry. However, there has been debate in recent years about the amount of recognition they are actually receiving. This led to the "#OscarsSoWhite" controversy in 2016 after two years passed without any African American representation in the four main acting categories at the Academy Awards. This controversy sparked a discussion about minority representation in films, and the 2017 Academy Awards ceremony reflected a renewed desire to showcase a diverse group of nominees.

The highest-grossing film nominated for Best Picture at the 2017 Academy Awards was *Hidden Figures*, which is about the black women who worked for NASA in the 1960s. This film marks an important step for blockbuster filmmaking for two reasons. First, it is a movie starring a group of African American women in a majority of the major roles. Furthermore, those roles are strong, and the characters are intelligent, self-sufficient, and relatable. Second, *Hidden Figures* is a mainstream movie that investigates America's historical racism that has long been ignored by films produced for a mainly white audience.

The Best Picture award winner in 2017 was *Moonlight*, a film specifically about the modern African American experience. It was the first film with an all-black cast to win this important award. Its victory represented a major milestone in the history of African Americans in film.

The unique and vibrant culture of African Americans has had a rocky history on the big screen. In the 21st century, it is finally possible for black people in the movie industry to reach their potential as creative artists. As the decades of the 2000s continue on, it is undoubted that African Americans will continue to shine on screen.

NOTES

Chapter One: Silent Movies, Loud Impact

1. Donald Bogle, *Toms, Coons, Mulattoes, Mammies & Bucks: An Interpretive History of Blacks in American Film*. New York, NY: Continuum, 2006, pp. 5–9.
2. Thomas Cripps, *Slow Fade to Black*. New York, NY: Oxford University Press, 1993, p. 29.
3. Bogle, *Toms, Coons, Mulattoes, Mammies & Bucks*, p. 10.
4. Quoted in Cripps, *Slow Fade to Black*, p. 52.
5. Quoted in Edward Mapp, *Blacks in American Films: Today and Yesterday*. Metuchen, NJ: Scarecrow, 1972, p. 19.
6. Quoted in Peter Noble, *The Negro in Films*. New York, NY: Arno, 1970, p. 47.
7. Quoted in Noble, *The Negro in Films*, p. 44.
8. Bogle, *Toms, Coons, Mulattoes, Mammies & Bucks*, p. 24.
9. Quoted in Noble, *The Negro in Films*, p. 33.

Chapter Two: The Rise of African Americans in Hollywood

10. Quoted in Cripps, *Slow Fade to Black*, p. 73.
11. Quoted in Cripps, *Slow Fade to Black*, p. 75.
12. Quoted in Cripps, *Slow Fade to Black*, p. 76.
13. Quoted in Arnie Bernstein, *Hollywood on Lake Michigan: 100 Years of Chicago and the Movies*. Chicago, IL: Lake Claremont, 1998, p. 46.
14. Quoted in Cripps, *Slow Fade to Black*, p. 84.
15. Cripps, *Slow Fade to Black*, p. 89.
16. Quoted in Cripps, *Slow Fade to Black*, p. 184.
17. "The Homesteader," *Chicago Defender*, February 22, 1919, p. 13.
18. Quoted in Cripps, *Slow Fade to Black*, p. 184.
19. Bogle, *Toms, Coons, Mulattoes, Mammies & Bucks*, p. 114.

Chapter Three: Still Serving on Screen

20. Quoted in Cripps, *Slow Fade to Black*, p. 237.
21. Quoted in Cripps, *Slow Fade to Black*, p. 242.
22. Quoted in Noble, *The Negro in Films*, p. 51.
23. Bogle, *Toms, Coons, Mulattoes, Mammies & Bucks*, p. 36.
24. Quoted in Cripps, *Slow Fade to Black*, p. 268.

25. Quoted in Bogle, *Toms, Coons, Mulattoes, Mammies & Bucks*, p. 59.
26. Quoted in Cripps, *Slow Fade to Black*, p. 361.
27. Quoted in Cripps, *Slow Fade to Black*, p. 364.
28. Bogle, *Toms, Coons, Mulattoes, Mammies & Bucks*, p. 98.
29. Quoted in Cripps, *Slow Fade to Black*, p. 387.

Chapter Four: The Film Industry and World War II

30. Quoted in Bogle, *Toms, Coons, Mulattoes, Mammies & Bucks*, p. 138.
31. Quoted in Thomas Cripps, *Making Movies Black: The Hollywood Message Movie from World War II to the Civil Rights Era*. New York, NY: Oxford University Press, 1993, p. 43.
32. Cripps, *Making Movies Black*, p. 43.
33. Quoted in Cripps, *Making Movies Black*, p. 50.
34. Quoted in Cripps, *Making Movies Black*, p. 54.
35. Quoted in Cripps, *Making Movies Black*, p. 46.
36. Quoted in Bogle, *Toms, Coons, Mulattoes, Mammies & Bucks*, p. 100.
37. Quoted in Bogle, *Toms, Coons, Mulattoes, Mammies & Bucks*, p. 129.
38. Cripps, *Making Movies Black*, p. 85.
39. Cripps, *Making Movies Black*, p. 68.
40. Bosley Crowther, "'Bataan,' Film of Heroic Defense of Peninsula, Starring Robert Taylor, Robert Walker and Thomas Mitchell, at Capitol," *New York Times*, June 4, 1943. www.nytimes.com/movie/review?res=9A0DE0DA1638E33BBC4C53DFB0668388659EDE&partner=Rotten%2520Tomatoes.
41. Cripps, *Making Movies Black*, p. 74.
42. Quoted in Cripps, *Making Movies Black*, p. 178.
43. Quoted in Bogle, *Toms, Coons, Mulattoes, Mammies & Bucks*, p. 136.
44. Quoted in Cripps, *Making Movies Black*, p. 190.
45. Quoted in Cripps, *Making Movies Black*, p. 192.
46. Cripps, *Making Movies Black*, p. 220.
47. Quoted in Bogle, *Toms, Coons, Mulattoes, Mammies & Bucks*, p. 144.

Chapter Five: Civil Rights and Hollywood Profits

48. Cripps, *Making Movies Black*, p. 250.
49. Quoted in Bogle, *Toms, Coons, Mulattoes, Mammies & Bucks*, p. 172.
50. Quoted in Cripps, *Making Movies Black*, p. 283.

51. Cripps, *Making Movies Black*, p. 284.

52. Quoted in Bogle, *Toms, Coons, Mulattoes, Mammies & Bucks*, p. 198.

53. Bosley Crowther, "Screen: Poitier Meets the Cockneys: He Plays Teacher Who Wins Pupils Over," *New York Times*, June 15, 1967. www.nytimes.com/movie/review?res=9E06E3DF103AE63ABC4D52DFB066838C679EDE.

54. Bosley Crowther, "Screen: 'Guess Who's Coming to Dinner' Arrives: Tracy-Hepburn Picture Opens at 2 Theaters The Cast," *New York Times*, December 12, 1967. www.nytimes.com/movie/review?res=9C03E6DE1430E23BBC4A52DFB467838C679EDE.

55. Clifford Mason, "Why Does White America Love Sidney Poitier So?" *New York Times*, September 10, 1967. www.nytimes.com/packages/html/movies/bestpictures/heat-ar.html.

56. Bogle, *Toms, Coons, Mulattoes, Mammies & Bucks*, p. 195.

Chapter Six: A New Era of Films

57. Quoted in George Alexander, *Why We Make Movies: Black Filmmakers Talk About the Magic of Cinema*. New York, NY: Harlem Moon, 2003, p. 23.

58. Jesse Algeron Rhines, *Black Film/White Money*. New Brunswick, NJ: Rutgers University Press, 1996, p. 43.

59. Rhines, *Black Film/White Money*, p. 43.

60. Quoted in Bogle, *Toms, Coons, Mulattoes, Mammies & Bucks*, p. 236.

61. Bogle, *Toms, Coons, Mulattoes, Mammies & Bucks*, p. 239.

62. Charles Harpole, *History of the American Cinema*. New York, NY: Scribner, 1990, p. 219.

Chapter Seven: Spike Lee and a New Wave of Motion Pictures

63. Roger Ebert, "Do the Right Thing," *Chicago Sun-Times*, June 30, 1989. rogerebert.suntimes.com/apps/pbcs.dll/article?AID=/19890630/REVIEWS/906300301/1023.

64. Quoted in Melvin Donalson, *Black Directors in Hollywood*. Austin, TX: University of Texas Press, 2003, p. 153.

65. Donalson, *Black Directors in Hollywood*, p. 244.

66. Amy Taubin, "Come On In, the Mainstream's Fine," *Village Voice*, October 19, 1999. www.village-voice.com/film/come-on-in-the-mainstreams-fine-6420720.

67. Janet Maslin, "Review/Film; Looking to the Dead for Mirth and Inspiration," *New York Times*, July 13, 1990. www.nytimes.com/movie/review?_r=1&res=9C0CE2DB1439F930A25754C0A966958260.

68. Rita Kempley, "What's Love Got to Do with It?," *Washington Post*, June 11, 1993. www.washingtonpost.com/ wp-srv/style/longterm/movies/ videos/whatslovegottodowith- itrkempley_a0a391.htm.

69. Roger Ebert, "Eve's Bayou," *Chicago Sun-Times*, November 7, 1997. www.rogerebert.com/reviews/ eves-bayou-1997.

Chapter Eight: The 2000s and Beyond

70. Quoted in Scott Bowles, "Black actors' Breakthrough Year," *USA Today*, February 6, 2005. usatoday30.usatoday.com/life/ movies/news/2005-02-06-black- actors_x.htm.

71. Quoted in Bowles, "Black Actors' Breakthrough Year."

72. Quoted in The Associated Press, "Africa's Ready for its Hollywood Closeup," Today, October 23, 2006. www.today.com/ popculture/africas-ready-its- hollywood-closeup- wbna15389880.

73. Esther Iverem, *We Gotta Have It: Twenty Years of Seeing Black at the Movies, 1986–2006*, New York, NY: Thunder's Mouth Press, 2007, p. 219.

FOR MORE INFORMATION

Books

Berry, S. Torriano, and Venise T. Berry. *The 50 Most Influential Black Films: A Celebration of African-American Talent, Determination, and Creativity.* New York, NY: Citadel Press, 2001.
The authors' selections for the most groundbreaking and important African American films of all time are grouped by decade, beginning with the early years of film and going right up until the end of the 20th century.

Green, Tara T. *Presenting Oprah Winfrey, Her Films, and African American Literature.* New York, NY: Palgrave Macmillan, 2013.
Oprah Winfrey is one of the most successful and influential black entertainers of all time; this book outlines her career and focuses on her support of other African Americans in the film industry.

Lubasch, Arnold H. *Robeson: An American Ballad.* Lanham, MD: Scarecrow Press, 2012.
This in-depth biography of Paul Robeson details the life and acting career of this major African American star of the early days of cinema.

Ndounou, Monica White. *Shaping the Future of African American Film: Color-Coded Economics and the Story Behind the Numbers.* New Brunswick, NJ: Rutgers University Press, 2013.
This book takes an in-depth look at how African Americans in the film industry are affecting the way movies get made, both today and in the future.

Petty, Miriam J. *Stealing the Show: African American Performers and Audiences in 1930s Hollywood.* Oakland, CA: University of California Press, 2016.
This modern investigation of black actors in the early years of motion pictures outlines the important changes that took place during the 1930s with respect to African Americans in film.

Websites

Black Film Center/Archive (www.indiana.edu/~bfca/home)
This website is a portal into Indiana University at Bloomington's wealth of resources regarding African Americans and film, including special collections and primary sources.

From Blackface to Blaxploitation: Representations of African Americans in Film (exhibits.library.duke.edu/exhibits/show/africanamericansinfilm)
Hosted by Duke University, this website has several pages that provide a detailed overview of the history of African Americans in film, including short articles about various eras.

History of African-Americans in Film (www.today.com/id/34246559/ns/today-today_entertainment/t/history-african-americans-film/#.WJikJLYrJBw)
This website features a detailed timeline of major events concerning black people in the film industry; it begins with 1915 and goes to 2008.

"How Racially Skewed Are the Oscars?" (www.economist.com/blogs/prospero/2016/01/film-and-race)
This article is a detailed analysis of the distribution of Academy Awards between black and white actors and motion picture professionals as of 2016; it contains charts and statistical evidence for the author's claims.

"Black Films Matter—How African American Cinema Fought Back Against Hollywood" (www.theguardian.com/film/2016/oct/13/do-the-right-thing-how-black-cinema-rose-again)
This detailed article showcases some of the high—and low—points for African Americans in film, including how the industry can grow even more equal in the future.

INDEX

PICTURE CREDITS

ABOUT THE AUTHOR

Camille R. Michaels has held many jobs throughout her life, including insurance agent, hotel clerk, and receptionist at a doctor's office. She earned her accounting degree from Cornell University and now helps people prepare their taxes. In her free time, she enjoys trying new restaurants, learning about history, and going dancing. She currently lives in Bowling Green, Ohio, with her husband and their Jack Russell terrier. This is her first book for young adults.